99 Ways to be Happier Every Day

99 Ways to be Happier Every Day

Terry Hampton & Ronnie Harper

PELICAN PUBLISHING COMPANY

Gretna 1999

First printing, 1997
First Pelican edition, 1999

Library of Congress Cataloging-in-Publication Data

Hampton, Terry.
    Ninety-nine ways to be happier every day / Terry Hampton
& Ronnie Harper. — 1st Pelican ed.
       p. cm.
    ISBN 1-56554-662-8 (pbk. : alk. paper)
    1. Happiness. 2. Conduct of life. I. Harper, Ronnie.
II. Title.
BJ1481.H215 1999
170'.44—DC21   99-32346
                                        CIP

Printed in the United States of America

Published by Pelican Publishing Company, Inc.
1000 Burmaster Street, Gretna, Louisiana 70053

Acknowledgements

We gratefully acknowledge everyone who has helped us in any way from the formulation of ideas to the actual completion of this project. Ronnie's wife, Tammie, and Terry's husband, Allen, along with Allen and Terry's daughter, Tracy are at the top of the list for putting up with all of our wild dreams (which are finally coming true) and for being the inspiration for many of our happy stories. They also sat through the very first time we performed our motivational presentation, and they didn't give up on us even after that! Judy Bowles is our good friend and best encourager. She and Dana Johnston helped immensely with the first draft of the manuscript. Marideth, who is full of wonderful, happy stories, will recognize a couple of tales she's told over the years. Bill Spencer gave us a really great idea which was a springboard for the title. All of our old and new friends at the Avenue Theatre have given us inspiration and some really great roles to play over the years, and we're forever grateful.

These are just a few of the people who have helped make us very happy!

Contents

Dedicated to the
serious pursuit of happiness.

Introduction

How and why does one *seriously* pursue happiness? We propose the why as follows: *As Americans, we're guaranteed the right in the Declaration of Independence!* When the founding fathers of the United States were drafting the document by which they were proclaiming this country's freedom from British rule, they held "these truths to be self-evident, that all men are created equal, that they are endowed by their Creator with certain unalienable Rights, that among these are Life, Liberty, and the PURSUIT OF HAPPINESS."

This does not guarantee happiness; it guarantees our right to pursue (and ultimately find) happiness.

So, *how* do we pursue happiness? That was the question we asked ourselves. To find the answers, we both made a list of things that made us and those around us happy. Then we rearranged and added to our combined lists until this book and the presentation that we do were born.

Please be warned, we don't claim to have any special credentials for this undertaking, other than the level of happiness which we have obtained in our own lives. And claiming to have achieved happiness doesn't mean we're cheery and all smiles every second of every day, but we do like ourselves and we love being alive.

Happiness may mean different things to different people, and there are obviously many components in the happiness equation. Some of those components we can control, others we cannot. For example, there are physiological and psychological factors that can't be changed. Scientists who study such things are now saying that we are born with about fifty percent of our ability to be happy, and we're in control of the other fifty percent. *That* is the fifty percent we're writing about in this book; the part which can be controlled.

Using stories, anecdotes and illustrations where possible, we look at some of the areas in life which all of us make decisions about every day. We approach the subject with the belief that anybody can be happier if he or she chooses to be.

Just like the Declaration of Independence, we can't guarantee your happiness, but we *can* encourage you to SERIOUSLY, HONESTLY, SINCERELY, WHOLEHEARTEDLY pursue it.

Order up a big helping of HAPPINESS from life's menu!

Chapter One

Check Your Attitude

If the three most important things in real estate are location, location, location, then the three most important things in determining your happiness must be

> *attitude,*
> > *attitude,*
> > > *attitude.*

1. Love living.

Love life! Savor every minute.

There's not enough that can be said about loving life. It is one of the most important things a person can do to achieve happiness. We must love the feelings, the smells, the sights, the sounds, and the challenges of life.

Have you ever watched a baby when it's not hungry or in need of a nap or diaper change? Babies love life. You can see joy practically ooze out of their pores, and it's definitely evident in the way their eyes sparkle and their tiny bodies can't stop moving. They're alive! And they're so happy just to be able to exist.

Oh sure, you say, it's easy for babies to be happy, they don't have to worry about the mortgage payment, and they don't have to get up every day and go to work. That's true. However, they live in the same world we do; they just happen to see it from a *different perspective.*

For a baby, an ant on the sidewalk provides occasion enough to stop and ponder a while. A fresh-washed blanket still warm from the dryer is too good to be true. A kitten is practically a miracle in how wonderful it is. Babies just haven't learned yet all of the things that are supposed to be unenjoyable. They learn from adults over the years that some things are done grudgingly by observing how we approach certain tasks and whether or not we enjoy doing those tasks.

When you wake up every morning, think about all the possibilities a new day brings. See the potential. When day-to-day living starts to become ho-hum, realize that there is life in every detail around you.

Enjoy the stars at night. Watch the sunset and see it rise. Look for beauty and new opportunities in the changing seasons.

Be careful not to let all the pleasures of living get lost in the shuffle of your own busy-ness. Remember that you love life, and let it help you be happy.

2. Have a sense of humor.

Allow yourself to laugh. Laugh easily. Laugh often. Laugh heartily. Laugh until you puke. (Well, that may be a little *too* much of a good thing.)

The importance of having a good sense of humor cannot be overstated. There are many things in the world which are sad, and if we dwell on them, there are too many reasons to be unhappy. We must decide to laugh.

Think again about babies and their outlook on life and consider this: it's estimated that on the average, children laugh 113 times each day. For adults, the average drops to just 11 times a day. Perhaps it's time to awaken the child in each of us!

A sense of humor can help get a person through tough situations. It can make seemingly impossible circumstances possible. It can make a gloomy outlook bright. It can make a job a better place to work. It can make relationships more fun and interesting. When people are asked what kind of person they're looking for to marry, one of the most frequent answers is "a person with a sense of humor."

Here are a couple of ground rules:

1. We must not laugh at inappropriate times or hurt the feelings of those around us with our laughter.

2. We should always be ready to laugh at ourselves. All of us make mistakes that are sometimes funny, and we shouldn't get upset if people laugh when we goof up! Laugh along with them.

Face it, it's funny if you go into a fast food restaurant and mistakenly ask for 'a frall order of smies.' (A friend of ours did that one time.)

We know a woman who hurriedly dressed for a wedding and ended up wearing one blue shoe and one brown shoe. And that's not the least of it; one was a high heeled shoe, and the other one was a flat! (Her son is still laughing about that incident.)

If you laugh, you *will* be happier because a merry heart is *good medicine!*

3. Take responsibility for your life and your actions.

A huge barrier to happiness is the tendency to constantly blame others for the way our lives are. But even if we *have* been mistreated and wronged, that's no excuse to be unhappy and to be a failure. Life just simply isn't fair; each of us must learn this truth and then get beyond it.

No matter how bad life may have been until now, it is within our power to change our circumstances by our actions. We can't wait for someone else to do it because it will never happen. The *choices* we make in life determine our level of happiness. This is proven by the fact that those who have been beaten down time and time again by tragic circumstances or disaster are often the ones who keep picking themselves up and trying again. They refuse to give up until they are successful, and usually, they refuse to stop there, but determine that they must also help those around them climb to the top. It's not what happens to us in life that counts; it's how we *react* to what happens that truly matters.

In addition to the things which happen to us at the hands of others, are the choices we make ourselves. Each choice has a consequence: some are good, some are bad. If we make good choices, and good things happen, we can *enjoy the consequences* of our decisions. And if we make poor choices, we must realize that we'll have to face the resulting *unpleasant* consequences. Many of the bad things that we would like to blame on someone else are simply a result of our own poor judgment.

We know an elementary school teacher who, while on playground duty, makes the kids who break the rules sit down on the sidewalk. The kids sit and whine about having to miss recess. He simply tells them, "If you can't do the time, don't do the crime."

We all know that breaking a playground rule isn't a crime, but what a great lesson for children to learn. They need to know there are consequences to every behavior. If we don't want to sit on the sidewalk, we can't push others on the playground! When we learn to take responsibility for our behavior, we find it easier to take responsibility for our happiness.

4. Be flexible.

We are indeed creatures of habit. We have routines; and if there is a change in these routines, it can ruin our day if we let it. The key to overcoming this problem is flexibility.

Change *can* be good. And sometimes, it is neither good nor bad; it merely happens. Whether we agree with a particular change or not, we shouldn't be prepared to hang onto things just because "that's the way it's always been."

The world is moving forward at a rapid pace, and change is around us every day. How well we adapt to that change will have a huge affect on our happiness. You see, it really doesn't matter if we like it or not, things will be different next year than they are now. For that matter, things will be different tomorrow than they are today! We can gripe if we want; that won't stop change. (But it will make us, and everyone around us, miserable.)

We've known people who immediately start to complain when someone brings up a new idea. They haven't had time to give the new idea any thought or consideration, but if it means having to change, then they've already decided it must be a bad idea.

If something changes, look at the change. Ask yourself, "Is it really something to get agitated over? Does this have long-term negative effects?" Most of the time you'll find change is okay. So, be flexible! Go with the change!

Not adapting to change is deadly in business, and it kills happiness just as surely.

Having said all of that, we've covered the number two dictionary definition of *flexible*. But the number one definition of *flexible* is one we like even better: *able to bend easily without breaking.*

Does bending your will to allow for different opinions to be heard cause you to break? Is it difficult for you to accept others who have views different from your own?

No one can have his or her way all of the time. Even when we really, really are right, we still may not get our way! Be ready to give in every now and then, and don't insist that everyone share your opinion. It's just not realistic, and you're setting yourself up for serious frustrations.

There are many, many situations which we tend to insist must go our way which are really of no consequence. Don't fuss about the little stuff. Save effort and time by sometimes letting someone else be in control of the details. It can actually be quite a relief.

Also, keep in mind that a satisfactory final outcome to a situation can usually be achieved in several ways. What difference does it make if the details used to reach the conclusion were our details or someone else's?

There are, however, rare times when you should not be flexible. These are the times when your principles are at stake. To give in would compromise your beliefs, and your *unhappiness* would be the result. Now, remember, don't try to use principles as a cover for opposing every new idea or trying to win every argument, but always stand up for the things which are truly important to you.

Terry relates a story about an issue of flexibility in her family:

"Before our daughter was born, Allen and I went through the usual, 'what are we going to name our child' discussions. We were immediately interested in family names, but a lot of them on my side of the family had already been used by my three sisters who had a total of thirteen children. And to be quite honest, Allen and I both thought that some of the family names on both sides were a little too old-fashioned for a child born in 1981. (Of course, if it came right down to it, I could have lived with any of the names on *my* side of the family, and Allen would have been just fine with the names from *his* side.)

"When we couldn't agree on a name from either side of the family, flexibility saved the day. We started using combinations of letters from the available family names, and finally came up with names we really liked. For a boy, instead of 'Randolph Deward' (a name we considered early on which incorporated the middle names of both our fathers), we decided on Joshua Cole.

Joshua was a name we liked, and Cole came from the first two letters of my father-in-law's first name, Coy, and the second two letters of my father's name, who is also an Allen.

"For a girl, we picked Tracy Eran. Tracy was a name on which we could agree, and the unusual spelling spelling of Eran was a result of choosing the second two letters of my mother's name, Fern, and the second two letters of Allen's mother's name, Wanda.

"I realize that seems like a long, convoluted route to use, but it really did make us feel as though we had accomplished our original goal of using family names, and we were both happy with the choices.

"Flexibility came into play again, when our daughter was born, and we were trying to decide whether to call her by her first name or her middle name. To hear Allen tell the story, he says, 'I wanted to call her Tracy, and Terry wanted to call her Eran, so we compromised and called her Eran!'

"I guess that is the way it was, because we did call her Eran which is what I wanted to do. But then, when she was about 13 years old, she decided she wanted to be known as Tracy. Even though by then all of our friends and family (including Allen) were quite happy calling her Eran, we decided it was an issue we needed to be flexible about because it was important to her and really had no long-term negative consequences.

"But I do have to add, we're *still* trying to get accustomed to the change!"

It isn't always easy being flexible — it may even hurt sometimes!

5. Be sincere.

Ah, sincerity. How welcome it is to find a friend, an associate – anyone, who is sincere. Sincerity doesn't equal a serious and somber, non-smiling outlook on life. It means living free from pretense or deceit. It means being honest, true and real in every regard. What you see is what you get. There is not a different face for every occasion and circumstance. There is no need to impress certain people because of their station in life. There is no looking down on others who don't measure up to whatever our standards might be.

Being sincere helps us be happy because we accept ourselves and those around us. We don't feel the need to pretend to be something we're not. We don't have to worry about trying to remember how we acted the last time we were in the presence of certain people. We're always the same, and it *simplifies life tremendously.*

So many people have been trapped into thinking they must live up to certain material standards. Shallow lifestyles, whether centered around expensive cars and designer clothes or whatever a person's particular distraction might be, are very unsatisfying. (Please don't classify everyone who has a nice car or a big house in this category. Having those things does not mean someone is shallow. It is a person's attitude and attachment toward material things that lead to real problems.)

If you've found yourself constantly desiring to acquire more and more "things," and you're not ever content regardless of how much you have, take a step back and reassess your values. Do you seek sincerity above worldly goods? We hope so because sincerity is a key to true happiness.

Be ready with a heartfelt smile. Offer to give real help. Have a genuine desire not to play games with the emotions of others. Shake hands with Terry's mom sometime and discover what a *sincere handshake* feels like. When we approach a situation with sincerity, we can almost never go wrong. People sense sincerity, and they appreciate it.

6. Decide to serve instead of be served.

Oh, how wonderful it is to imagine lying around all day on satin sheets and velvet pillows being waited on by servants attending to our every whim and desire. It might be fun for a few days, but eventually, for most of us, something inside would be seeking something different, something more satisfying. The idea of being served and not providing service to others in return is contrary to every principle of happiness.

Have you ever noticed those around you who have fallen into the habit of constantly complaining because they're not receiving the treatment they feel they deserve? They're so focused on making sure their rights are not violated, and that they're getting credit for everything they do that they can't seem to enjoy themselves anymore. Even volunteers in some organizations forget why they're doing what they're doing and start seeking recognition for their efforts above the satisfaction of helping others.

We must seek for ourselves *only* the satisfaction of helping others, and maintain a helpful attitude in everything we do. We should learn not to walk past a task that needs doing just because it's "someone else's" job. Terry gives an example:

"I'm reminded of the towel dispenser at my former place of business. In the restroom, which was shared by about ten people, there was a roll towel dispenser. You've probably seen similar ones in public restrooms. It's the kind that generally has either a white or blue linen towel hanging down in a loop under the dispenser. If you look inside, you'll see that as the towel is used, it rolls onto the 'used towel rod.' When the entire roll runs through the dispenser, it is taken out and sent to the cleaners, and a fresh roll has to be installed.

"If you've ever seen one of these dispensers that has run a towel through the whole cycle, you'll see a little message printed on the dispenser that says, 'Ask attendant to install clean towel.' Well, at our business we didn't have a restroom attendant, so it fell to those of us who worked there and used the restroom to change the towel as needed.

"Sometimes, it worked out that I would go in to wash my

hands, and I'd pull out the last little bit of towel on the roll creating the need to install a fresh towel. At other times, I'd walk into the restroom and see that the towel had run out, and nobody had taken the time to put in a fresh one. Eventually, it got to the point that every time I put a fresh towel in that dispenser, I would think to myself, *I'm the only one who ever changes this stupid towel.* It would be extremely aggravating to change a towel that someone else should have already changed, because it only takes a couple of minutes, and it's not difficult to do. Occasionally, I wouldn't change the towel either, leaving it for the next person to do.

"Gradually, I began to realize that maybe everyone who installed a fresh towel thought he or she was the only one who ever had to do it, and that they probably didn't enjoy the task. (At least one other person told me she felt that way.)

"I thought, isn't it odd that such a little task can affect people so negatively? And doesn't selfish thinking slip into our minds in small and subtle ways? If it's not a towel dispenser, it's some other minor thing. I finally decided to change the towel ungrudgingly and be happy to help every time I did it. I'm still learning about serving others, but just making that decision made the whole experience completely different. I smiled and thought of the conscious decision I had made to help (even though it was in a very small way) instead of complain every time I changed the towel."

We suggest, that you wake up every morning and say to yourself, 'How many people am I going to help today?'

Then, try not to draw attention to yourself and your good deeds. If you've never done anonymous deeds of kindness for others, try it sometime! The happiness it brings far outweighs a brief pat on the back when you brag on yourself.

Serving others is not a lowly position. It is, in fact, in our careers, in our homes or as volunteers, the highest calling we can have. It is the only reason a person should ever go to his job and the only reason anyone should ever be in business. We shouldn't do any job just for the money. (If our priority is to serve others, the money will come.) We must do it because we want to serve.

Arthur F. Sheldon, writer of the motto for Rotary International puts it like this, *"He profits most who serves best."*

7. Recognize that no one owes you anything in life.

To truly accomplish being servants in life, we must get it inside our heads and our hearts that no one – not our parents, not our children, not our spouse, none of our relatives, not the government – that is *no one* owes us anything!

Just because we are wonderful people and had the good fortune to be born does not mean we are entitled to a free ride in life. So many problems, so much bitterness can be avoided when people stop looking for an easy way out.

Crazy, multi-million dollar lawsuits that should never even have been initiated make it to court and *win*. They are by-products of people who are rampantly seeking some way to achieve the new "American dream." Not the dream that hard work and perseverance can pay off, but that a lucky break at someone else's expense is all a person needs to get ahead in life.

A person will never be happy if he's always dissatisfied with his lot in life. And we'll always be dissatisfied if we look to those around us to provide us with what we want and need.

If we constantly expect others to provide for our needs and wants, and we don't get what we're expecting, we're disappointed. This puts our happiness in the hands of others and not in our own where it belongs. When we *do* get what we feel like we're "owed," it's never appreciated because we're expecting it anyway.

Once we realize that no one owes us anything in life, we will be happier, and who knows, we may be pleasantly surprised when someone *does* give us something!

Everyone is responsible for getting his own slice of "American Dream" pie!

8. Be unselfish.

What must be at the very center of us is the idea that *self-less*ness equals happiness; *selfish*ness equals unhappiness. It's not enough to passively realize that no one owes us anything. We must actively and unselfishly give to others. Share our time, our resources, ourselves.

Even some who have given their lives to helping others are selfish with their possessions and with their time. Be careful that you are not so possessive of "your things" that those material things become more important than people. *Things are never more important than people and their needs.*

Unselfishness brings the freedom to truly enjoy life. Bringing joy into the lives of others is really the only way to bring it into your own life.

As the Olympic torch criss-crossed its way to Atlanta for the 1996 Summer Games, there were so many touching and heroic stories which emerged from the ranks of the torch-bearers. One particular story which we heard about was of a young man who was nominated for the honor because of an act of unselfishness.

It seems that this young man, who was a college student struggling to pay tuition and get through school, one day found a few hundred dollars in a parking lot. He turned in the money to the proper authorities and after it was not claimed, he was given the money to do with as he chose.

Even though a few hundred dollars was a lot of money, instead of keeping it, he decided to give it to a fund to help a boy who needed money for an expensive surgical procedure. He supposed that would be the end of the matter, but it was far from over. So much publicity was created about his generosity that the remaining money needed for the surgery was quickly raised, and the boy became a successful survivor of the condition which would have otherwise killed him. Then the young man was nominated by the boy's family for the honor of carrying the Olympic torch.

We never know how an unselfish act will change our lives or the lives of those around us.

9. Pettiness is not compatible with happiness.

What a personal pet peeve pettiness is for us! In fact, seeing the big picture in life was the main motivation for us to write this book, and it is the subject of the last chapter.

Those who are sold out to small-mindedness may be the only group not truly capable of being happy. Pettiness enables us to find fault even when there is not the slightest wrong thing about a person or a situation, and we simply cannot be happy when our attitude is one of finding fault and complaining and allowing trivial matters to take precedence in our lives.

There certainly are enough small problems out there that a person could spend his or her entire life focusing on them. The problem with focusing on the small issues is that we tend to never really accomplish anything. We should spend our time dealing with the big problems in life; there are enough big problems without wasting time focusing on the small ones.

Pettiness arises out of feelings of inferiority or habit. Neither reason is good. (Some people are so busy griping about the meaningless things that they forget to be happy.) Removing pettiness, spitefulness, and any other similar attitudes from our lives will help make us happier.

So, if you are petty, decide to stop it now! Don't live another minute without promising to change your attitude.

Make these vows as quickly as you can:

I will not intentionally do good deeds solely to be noticed by others.

Never again will I be consumed to distraction with the reasons why people do particular things or behave in certain ways.

I refuse to become less productive by constantly keeping track of what my co-workers or friends or family members are doing.

I won't tell and re-tell every little detail of my own personal life or what I might discover about the personal lives of others. Money, in particular my lack or abundance of it, will not be a topic of my casual conversations with friends and acquaintances.

I won't be a "tattle tale," telling insignificant things about the behavior of others hoping to make them look bad.

No longer will I work two hours balancing my checkbook because I'm trying to find the source of a twelve-cent error. My time is too valuable!

I'm going to stop letting negative things which I've merely heard about others have an affect on the way I feel about them.

I will not be a nitpicker or a nagger.

I will not harbor ill feelings.

I will seek to recognize those small and insignificant things which I have elevated to a high place in my life, and I will cast them down from their place of importance.

I WILL NOT BE PETTY!

No matter what the situation is –
my ATTITUDE is bigger and
stronger!

10. Complaining is a joy stealer.

Selfishness has lots of ugly faces, and complaining is one of the worst.

Why do people complain? Well, think about *what* they complain about. Here are a few complaints we've noticed people have: the weather (they're too hot or too cold); the news; their jobs (including bosses, co-workers, conditions, wages); their health; their lack of money; their relatives; politicians; taxes; other drivers on the highway; road construction; the postal service; their food at a restaurant; their neighbors; answering machines; the shape of their body; the way someone looked at them . . .

In short, a person can complain about two things: the things that he *can* change and the things that he *can't* do anything about. But either way, it's selfish to complain because in some way, something is not going exactly the way he wants it. Complaining is the main game at a pity party.

We can't do anything about the temperature, for example, so why not learn to enjoy it as much as possible, and dress appropriately. In fact, there are lots of things that we really can't change, so we should learn to accept those things and try to see them in the best light possible.

And many things which bother you that can't be changed (by you), can be avoided (by you). If you consistently get food you don't like at a particular restaurant, stop eating there!

Some things you *can* change. So try to change them if you want to, but don't complain! If you must express your opinion to someone to try to bring about a change, make sure you put a positive spin on what you're saying. People respond negatively to complaining.

Let's make a pact to complain less and compliment more.

Listening to complaints can be a real pain in the neck.

27

11. Decide that things which are beyond your control will not bother you.

We must decide that other people's actions and situations *will not* have a negative effect on us.

When we go somewhere (especially in a car), we're going to encounter other people doing stupid things. We must realize this in advance and tell ourselves that we're not going to let it bother us. Then, when it happens (a stupid thing), we have to remind ourselves of our promise and shrug it off. Our entire trip (and that of our passengers) will be much more enjoyable.

Terry notes that even though he's trying to improve, it's often agonizing to travel with her husband, Allen.

"Allen is an excellent driver, and his expectations of the abilities of others are quite high. People who don't pay attention to the road and don't know and obey driving rules and laws when they operate a vehicle really annoy him. Naturally, he shares a lot of his frustrations with his passengers. (Me, mostly.) He wants to write a book of driving tips which he thinks should be required reading for anyone before they obtain their driver's license. (At least that's what he says when he's being *nice*.)

"His attitude is getting better. *Occasionally*, he manages to drive all the way across town without comment!"

At least Allen doesn't let the *weather* have a negative effect on his attitude – something which does frustrate many people.

Terry explains her thoughts on the matter: "I've learned to enjoy almost every kind of weather. For example, since I've *decided* that I like rainy days, I've found that I *really do* enjoy the rain. In fact, my daughter's favorite weather is when it's rainy or cloudy. I like wintertime, too, and don't mind the cold weather. I've discovered that some people get almost angry when I tell them that! But hey, I figure that I can't change the weather, so I might as well make the best of it."

If we look for the positive in what seems to be negative, we will be happier. And if we set our minds to it, we can decide that minor setbacks (like a flat tire) will not ruin our whole day. No more "having a bad day"! Away with bad days forever.

Here's a note from Terry: When I showed Allen what I had written about him in this section, I asked him if it was okay for me to include it in the book. He laughed, and said yes, it was okay, but he thought he should get to include some driving tips! So here is a brief excerpt from what might be called "Rules of the Road According to Allen Hampton," (tongue-in-cheek version).

Terry and Ronnie were kind enough to give me a page in their book so that I could give their readers a few driving tips. At first, I told Terry that maybe it's not such a good idea to do this because her goal is to build people up, and mine is to bring them back down to the *seriousness* of driving. Plus, most people are evidently not bothered by other people's driving habits – maybe it's just me. So, this isn't to make you happier, it's to make *me* happier.

As I have been going over tip after tip in my mind, I keep thinking that one page isn't enough room (and now I've already used enough space for a couple of good tips!).

When I'm out driving, I'm easy to spot in my 1968 International Travellall, 4-wheel drive with a lift kit and monster tires. It's about 7½ foot from the ground to the roof line, flat black in color and soon to be zebra-striped (black and white) so everyone will notice it, I'm sure.

Here are a couple of the more important things that fellow drivers can do to make me happy. First, don't be in such a hurry that you have to tailgate. You will most likely see my brake lights come on, and then you'll just drive right underneath. (And you know that you can't pass from under there.)

Second, when you're in a long line of stopped traffic, please don't park on railroad tracks or block an intersection, because in case of an emergency, you may not be lucky enough to have someone like me to push you out of the way. (Believe me, there isn't much I can't move!) And driving a car that looks like an accordion can't be much fun for you.

Thank you for your attention and maybe one day when you see a 1968 International Travellall that stands over 7½ foot tall, painted like a zebra, you and I can exchange a wave and a smile, and we'll *both* be happier because of it!

12. Emotions should not rule your life.

Feelings and emotions are very important parts of who we all are, but we cannot be led by them every day.

Our feelings sometimes are not very practical. They can take us down roads that are deadends and cause us to make hasty decisions that we'll later regret. The old saying, "Fools rush in where angels fear to tread" comes to mind in this regard. And people who are continually doing foolish things are not happy.

We have so many emotions, good and bad: love, hate, fear, joy, sorrow. . . . And giving into those emotions while completely chucking reason and common sense out the window is not a good way to achieve happiness.

Channel your emotional side into thoughtful creativity. Follow your heart, but make sure you know your heart!

A happy life is one which is balanced. So we should try to balance our emotions with common sense, and try not to be tossed around by every breeze that blows by us. Always floating along with no highs or lows is a pretty boring way to live. But constantly darting here and there being led by one emotional crisis after another leaves people in such turmoil, that they never have *time* to be truly happy.

There are appropriate times for almost every emotion. To be sure, some are more productive than others, and the "positive" emotions are the ones we should all cultivate in ourselves. But fear, for example, is never necessary. (It is helpful to have a healthy amount of *respect* for tigers to avoid injury should you ever find yourself lost in the jungle. But don't be so afraid of tigers that you can't go to the zoo.)

Living a balanced life in all areas is a true key to happiness. We must master our emotions to bring our lives into balance. Have an outburst every now and then if you must, but not on a daily basis, please!

Our attitude should be that we will always approach life by looking at situations from a variety of viewpoints. Finding the right mix of emotions and practicality is a challenge worth the effort when we're seeking happiness.

Following is a short story which illustrates the danger of being led by feelings and emotions. It is titled "The Appointment in Samarra," and it was written by W. Somerset Maugham.

Death speaks: There was a merchant in Baghdad who sent his servant to market to buy provisions and in a little while the servant came back, white and trembling, and said, Master, just now when I was in the market-place I was jostled by a woman in the crowd and when I turned I saw it was Death that jostled me. She looked at me and made a threatening gesture; now, lend me your horse and I will ride away from this city and avoid my fate. I will go to Samarra and there death will not find me. The merchant lent him his horse, and the servant mounted it, and he dug his spurs in its flanks and as fast as the horse could gallop he went. Then the merchant went down to the marketplace and he saw me standing in the crowd and he came to me and said, Why did you make a threatening gesture to my servant when you saw him this morning? That was not a threatening gesture, I said, it was only a start of surprise. I was astonished to see him in Baghdad, for I had an appointment with him tonight in Samarra.

13. No one can make you angry. You allow yourself to become angry.

Life is frustrating. People are frustrating. It seems that there is always someone who has an attitude or even a comment which we simply cannot abide. Certain personalities drive us crazy. Co-workers have plans and ideas which are in direct opposition to our own. Our anger lashes out. And anger is an honest emotion; we all become angry from time to time.

But take note: *it is our anger*, and it is within our power to control anger in ourselves. We cannot control situations or how people behave, but we *can* learn to control our anger. And we're on the road to happiness when we find we no longer need to display anger in outbursts at every little situation.

"He makes me so angry!" How many times have you heard that (or said it)?

But it's not true. It's a simplistic statement, but correct to say *we* allow *ourselves* to become angry.

To help remedy this situation, we should try to become more accepting of the attitudes of others. Other people do have good ideas. If after considering those ideas, you still find yourself disagreeing with their opinions, do so without raising your voice (or your blood pressure).

Sometimes there are wrong attitudes which deserve to have anger directed at them: prejudice, hypocrisy, hate, etc. If we allow ourselves to be angry at those attitudes and that anger causes us to act in a way to bring about positive change, then that is a good use of anger. But we should always, as much as possible, try to direct our anger at attitudes rather than the people who are displaying those attitudes.

We should reserve our anger for only very serious issues and not make a habit of being angry every day. People who are *always* angry can never be happy.

Anger is momentary madness, so control your passion or it will control you.
Horace, *Epistles*

32

14. Worry is perhaps the most unproductive attitude of all.

When we decide that we'll not be bothered by things beyond our control, then we must also decide to *stop worrying* as we travel down the lumpy road of happiness. Worry does nothing to solve problems or remedy undesirable circumstances.

A preacher we know gives callers to his answering machine a word of wisdom about worry. He says it's like a rocking chair; it gives you something to do, but it doesn't get you anywhere.

Worry is similar to complaining in that you can really only worry about two things, and neither of them can be solved by worrying. The first situation is dwelling on something you can't change. The matter is something over which you have no control, but you worry about it anyway. This seems pretty obvious as you sit and think about it, but it happens all the time. People worry about the end of the world or maybe about a soap opera character's problem. Nothing can be done about either so why put time and energy into worrying about it?

The second situation is dwelling on a circumstance you *can* change. So often people sit around and worry about something which is in an area where they could make a difference, but instead of doing something about it, they waste time and energy worrying.

We know a woman whose daughter has cystic fibrosis. From the moment the girl was diagnosed with the disease, the mother became determined to do what she could to give her daughter the best therapy and help at home which could possibly be provided. In addition, the mother and several people in the community began hosting an annual concert to raise money to aid in research to find a cure. They've raised tens of thousands of dollars over the past several years, and there have been some important breakthroughs during that time. This is a woman who decided not to worry about her daughter's uncertain future, but instead meet the situation head on with hope and determination.

If you can do something about a situation, don't worry about it! *Do something.*

15. Be positive.

So, we've decided to stop worrying and complaining. What are we going to do with all that extra time? Here's an idea – let's spend our time maintaining a positive attitude toward life!

And we don't mean to be like one of Ronnie's students when he was told to "think positive." He said, "Mr. Harper, I'm *positive* I'm going to *flunk* this test!"

You must be optimistically positive.

Having a positive attitude doesn't just happen overnight; it's something that must be cultivated over a period of time.

Begin by starting each day with something positive. Find a book with inspirational sayings or stories and read it in the morning when you get up. It will help set the tone for the rest of the day. Whatever tone is set in the morning usually tends to be the tone for the whole day – we've all seen it happen with both positive and negative tones. Something happens in the morning that is negative, and you can't seem to shake that feeling the rest of the day. But if we make an effort to start the day on a positive note, we increase the chances that we'll have a positive approach to everything all day, and we'll be ready to jump into life's ups and downs as conquering heroes!

Deciding to be upbeat will help you have a new outlook on undesirable circumstances. You'll discover that you can change a whole situation around by just changing your attitude toward that situation because a positive attitude is contagious. One person who has decided to be positive can walk into a situation and set the tone for everyone involved. *You* can be that person if you make up your mind that you're going to be positive no matter what confronts you. Once you help set the positive tone, you and everybody around you can be happier.

16. Don't be a victim.

We've known many people who have allowed themselves to become victims by their own actions and attitudes. Sometimes you don't even have to get to know people to realize that they are victims. While checking out of a hotel one time, Terry encountered a victim. This woman wasn't being mugged or physically harmed in any way at the time, but she was a victim nonetheless.

"When I walked up to check out, there was a man being helped by the one clerk at the counter, and a woman was leaning against the wall at the end of the counter several feet away. She was accompanied by a small child and another woman. She had her elbow on the counter with her arm holding up her slumped over head. She looked like she had encountered some sort of problem, and since she was not in line behind the man checking out, I assumed she was being assisted by another clerk who was visible in the office behind the counter busily attending to something.

"I got in line behind the man to wait my turn. When he left, I stepped to the counter and told the clerk I was ready to check out. She started the process. After a slight pause, the woman said, not really to me or anyone else, but more or less just into the air, 'I thought I was next.'

"It was too late for her to go ahead at that point because the clerk, who also apparently didn't realize that the other woman should have been next, already had my information pulled up on the computer screen.

'I'm so sorry!' I exclaimed.

'Well. . .' she shrugged.

'No, really I am,' I said. 'I thought you were already being helped.'

'No, no. That's okay, I guess,' she mumbled, unsmiling and obviously aggravated.

"I apologized one more time as I walked away, and she

didn't acknowledge me. She no doubt had quite a conversation with her companion about that rude person who butted in line!

"Her attitude, her actions, her body language all screamed out that this woman was a victim."

We shouldn't strive to aggressively and rudely exert our opinions and always try to get our way, but we should not become victims by our passivity.

How easy it would have been for her to confidently take her place in line. That would have taken care of the misunderstanding right from the start. If she was too tired or sick to stand in line and needed the extra support of a wall and her elbow, all she had to do was quietly step to the counter as the gentleman was leaving, and let everyone know it was her turn.

This is a simple and perhaps insignificant example of how a person can allow herself to be a victim. So many of life's disappointments are brought on by our own attitudes. But even if a situation occurs which is truly beyond our control, and we suffer because of it, remember it's not what happens to us in life that really matters; it's how we *react* to what happens to us.

The victim in this story didn't smile very much that day; she didn't look like she was much accustomed to being happy.

Are *you* going to choose to be a victim, or are you going to choose to be happy?

17. Be confident.

Confident people are usually happy people. Always be ready to go forward without fear, and don't hold back. Confidence gives you courage. If you're confident in yourself, you will not allow the negative things that others may say about you have an adverse effect on your life. You shrug off the bad things and accept with modesty the good things people say about you.

Lack of confidence makes people miserable. It leads to statements like:

"I wish I had tried for that promotion, but I knew I'd never get it."

"I'll probably never get married. I'm just not good looking."

"Why should I even try to learn how to play the guitar; I'll never be any good."

"If only I were . . ."

"I'm not good enough to . . ."

"I'll never be able . . ."

Oh, how many wonderful opportunities we miss out on in life because of a lack of confidence!

We won't try new things because we're afraid we might fail, and as a result it seems we always have some excuse for not bettering ourselves. We must always have an attitude that says, "I can do it!" That change in attitude alone can change our lives in so many ways.

Do you think the duo of Ronnie and Terry would have ever come into being if either one of us lacked confidence? No way! We met in the first place because both of us had the nerve to become involved in community theatre. Ask anyone who's ever done it; it takes a lot of confidence to get up on stage and do live theatre, especially in front of your friends and family in your hometown!

And even though both of us realized for a long time what our calling in life is, without a big dose of confidence we never would have dreamed that we could actually become paid professional speakers and writers. We're just "regular folks." Nothing really extraordinary has ever happened to either one of us by the usual standards, but here we are!

You can have that same level of confidence in everything you approach in your life. For example, if there's an opening where you work which is a promotion for you, go for it! Even if you fail, you have nothing to lose by trying. Your life will not be worse than before, and you stand at least some chance of making it significantly better.

To help you gain confidence, put 110% effort into everything you do. Your list of accomplishments will grow, and your sincere enthusiasm will eventually be rewarded.

If you're a single person sitting at home all the time who would rather be around people, stop making excuses and get out there and meet someone. You may not think you're good looking, but we bet you're wrong. And you know what? Even if you are not attractive by the whacked out standards of society, have you looked around you? The world is full of unattractive people! (And most of them are not so much physically unattractive as they are "attitudinally" unattractive.)

We must be careful never to cross the line between confidence and arrogance; it is a fine line. Knowing we can do anything must never turn us into know-it-all personalities. Arrogance causes us to start thinking we're better than other people, and none of us are really any better than anyone else. We should take others along with us in our confidence instead of leaving them behind in the dust. As we successfully conquer one mountain after another, we must not do it at the expense of those around us.

Look at the areas in your own life in which you feel held back, then break loose from those bonds with confidence, and a promise to yourself that you'll never again say, "I can't do that."

You can do anything!

18. "I can" vs. "I.Q."

Henry Ford once said whether you think you can or you think you can't, you are right. Your attitude is more important than your skill level or your I.Q. It all comes down to the "I can" vs. "I.Q." mentality.

There are many who are underachievers in life; talented people who are doing nothing but sitting at home watching television. Ronnie tells the story of a former student of his:

"I knew a student who had an above average I.Q. He had a great vocabulary and knew the meaning of almost any word. He had the potential to be anything he wanted to be. He had one serious problem (besides being arrogant); he lacked the self-discipline to get up and come to school. He stayed up all night and watched television or played on his computer. He finally missed so much school that it was impossible to get caught up, and he quit. He wasted the intelligence and the gifts he was given. He might have cured cancer or AIDS. With his ability, he might have been the next William Shakespeare or Ernest Hemingway, but we'll never know.

"Do you have talent that you're wasting?

"On the other hand, there are also overachievers. People who have average I.Q. and abilities who become doctors, scientists, and entrepreneurs. One of the best music teachers I have ever encountered could not play the piano 'like other music teachers.' She often told the story of her senior year in college and her piano finals. After she played her final for her teacher, he said, 'I'm going to pass you on one condition. You must promise me you will never take money from others for piano lessons.' Anxious to graduate, she made the promise and went on to teach music in the public schools.

"She has taught for over 20 years now, and her choirs have become known for their sight reading abilities. This was attributed to her poor piano playing skills. She could not play the parts 'like other music teachers' so her students had to be able to read the music and stay on their parts. Her choirs have also received

"1" ratings for over 20 years straight at state music competitions. They have performed in several countries including Great Britain, Austria and Russia.

"She has touched the lives of thousands as a teacher and thousands more as a director of some great choirs. What would have happened if she had given up on becoming a music teacher because she couldn't play a piano "like other music teachers"? Where would those thousands of students be? I can tell you that you wouldn't be reading this because I am one of those students she touched."

An underachiever, an overachiever, a quitter or a fighter, which are you? Which do you want to be? The choice is yours and yours alone, but there are those who say you owe it to yourself and everyone around you to make the best of what you've been given.

People owe this marvelous world whatever talents they can give it. They owe enough to the world to be a part of it, to use their talents to make others happy.

- Mary Martin

YES,
you
can
climb
all
the
way
to
the
top!

19. Like your work.

To help yourself achieve this goal, first you must choose a job or career that you really want to do. Take an assessment of what your strengths and weaknesses, likes and dislikes are, and then match your talents to your occupation. If you're married (whether you're the husband or the wife), perhaps you'll determine that you're best suited for staying home and taking care of your house and family. That's great! None of us should feel pressured to "get a job" just because "it's the thing to do."

When you have a career (inside or outside your home) that suits you, always make sure that you take pride in your work. Do your best to do your best! If you start to feel unhappy and out of sorts, remember all the good reasons you first decided to do what you're doing.

However, don't let your career become your only focus in life. This leads to burn out and ulcers, not happiness. Don't be a workaholic, spending almost every waking moment at the office or scrubbing your kitchen floor. True enjoyment in your work will definitely help you achieve happiness, but make sure your career doesn't become more important than your family or your social life.

When you're hired to do a job, remember why you were hired and for what job you were hired. If you were hired to pick up trash, don't complain when you're asked to pick up trash. We hear some people always complaining about their jobs: a waitress who says, "I hate cleaning up after people" or a teacher who complains, "I hate being around kids all day." What do you suppose they expected their jobs to be like?

Ronnie tells the story of one of his students who took a job at Wal-Mart:

> This young man's job was to push carts in from the parking lot. After a week, he came to school complaining about his boss telling him he

had to go to the end of the parking lot and get a cart that a customer had left.

I asked him, "What is your job?"

He said, "To push in carts."

"Did they say that you would only be pushing in carts that were left close to the building?" I asked.

"No," he said.

Then I said to him, "What are you complaining about? When you take a job as a cart pusher, *you're going to be pushing in carts!*"

This is easy to see when it's somebody else's job; the trick is to recognize it in our own jobs. If we're hired to do a job, any job, we should *do it* instead of standing around complaining about the work.

If you find you're working some place that you'd rather not be, you can do two things. You can either try to make the best of it (it could be that your attitude toward your work is poor), or if you're really certain your current job is just not for you, move on.

Sometimes, out of economic necessity, or for whatever reason, people feel forced to do work they do not enjoy. While each of us who are true seekers of happiness should be able to "bloom where we're planted," and find some degree of happiness in almost every situation, it is indeed difficult to be happy when you wake up every morning dreading the work day ahead and watching the minutes and hours drag by at an agonizingly slow pace once you've arrived.

If you're not truly happy with your job, it isn't worth staying there. You aren't helping anybody: not your boss, not yourself. Life is too short to spend it doing a job which you do not like.

Whatever you do, make sure you do your best — and enjoy it!

20. Love yourself, then you can love others.

This seems like a very simple concept, and it is!

Our highest calling is to love others as we love ourselves. Loving oneself is so often neglected because of low self-esteem, the desire to be unselfish, or even well-meaning parents in our youth who wouldn't tell us we were pretty or handsome or smart because they didn't want us to get a "big head."

If you think there's something wrong with loving yourself, you've got another think coming! It's not only okay to love yourself, it's a *mandatory requirement*. Lack of love for ourselves prevents so many of us from finding true happiness.

We know a man who is intelligent, funny, witty, a great conversationalist, and extremely talented in many areas, but he has not learned to love himself. He has so much to offer those around him, but he's limited himself by his feelings of inadequacy. He could truly be an inspiration and a role model, but because he has not learned the concept of self love, he restricts how much he can give others. This attitude interferes with every aspect of his life from his love life to his profession.

It also doesn't take much to get him down, and he's always worried about what others will think or say about him. He's definitely not as happy as he could be.

We don't know what happened in his life that gave him the idea he's not worth loving, but we do know for him to be truly happy and have the ability to love others, he's going to have to realize that he's worthy of love. He must learn how to love himself.

We can tell him what a great job he does and what a wonderful person he is (and we do tell him those things), but the self love must come from within *him*.

Part of loving yourself means that you realize you deserve happiness, and you deserve to be taken care of. This does not mean you put yourself before all others, but it does mean that you have to take care of yourself so you will be healthy – mentally and physically. If you take care of yourself, you will be in better condition to help others.

You're really a wonderful person. A uniquely individual human being. You're special, and no one can take your place. You have your faults, but so do the rest of us. Strive daily to overcome your shortcomings and concentrate on your strengths and talents. When you mess up, forgive and ask to be forgiven and go on with your life.

Okay, so it's starting to sound like "Daily Affirmations with . . ." But, doggone it, you really are deserving of being loved. You also deserve to be happy no matter what anybody has told you. Isn't it about time you *let* yourself be happy?

Please keep in mind, however, that we can't love ourselves exclusively. Happiness doesn't begin and end with us and how we feel about ourselves. Instead, we learn to love ourselves as a training ground for loving others. After we love ourselves, then we're able to love others with such unselfishness that it will take our relationships to new heights of happiness.

When we are able to truly and unconditionally love those around us, that is when real happiness has arrived in our lives.

I love me –
just the way I am!

21. Happiness is an attitude.

We must *decide* that we will be happy because happiness, just like unhappiness, is a choice and an attitude. There are some people who have decided that they're *not* going to be happy, no matter what happens. Something positive will take place in their lives, and they're still unhappy.

We must decide to let ourselves be happy. If something positive happens to us, we should embrace it and accept it. It's okay to be happy. It's okay to be happy even if others around us don't seem to be happy. Remember, each person has to make that choice for himself.

Another way to look at it is that we are only going to be as happy as we allow ourselves to be. Abraham Lincoln said, "Most folks are about as happy as they make up their minds to be." This is so true! Each person has to handle his or her own trials and tribulations. How we handle those problems determines our level of happiness. Life can be as bad or as good as we want it to be.

But we must also have realistic goals when it comes to happiness. There will be times when we're not happy. We're going to have to deal with our friends and family members dying or getting sick. There will be days when we get up, and we won't feel like being happy. The trick is to feel the way we feel, then deal with that feeling. Don't go around trying so hard to be happy that it makes you miserable.

Angela, a character on the television series *My So Called Life* said, "I think that if my mother didn't work so hard at being happy, she would actually be happy."

We must be careful not to get so caught up in trying to look the happy look or talk the happy talk that we forget to be happy. Sometimes all it takes to be happy is *remembering* to be happy.

Whatever your circumstance, remember to be happy.

Chapter Two

Communicate Skillfully

Even though we should always try to express ourselves very clearly, so as to avoid confusion and misunderstanding, there is so much more to communication than just talking.

> *We must be*
> *very careful*
> *how we use*
> *the words*
> *we say...*

22. Be honest with yourself and others.

Communicating in an honest and forthright manner saves you so much trouble and heartache!

Have you ever known someone who told so many different lies to so many different people that they couldn't remember which lie they had told and to whom? You can certainly have some interesting conversations with someone like that, but spending a lot of time with them isn't much fun.

People who lie are unhappy; happy people know that keeping track of all those lies takes too much time and effort! Everyone can use a good dose of honesty.

Ronnie tells the story of a student who had trouble telling the truth:

"This student was not happy with her life so she created her own reality. She would tell a lie, and when anyone asked her about it, she created another lie to cover the first one. This would go on until she was so over her head in lies that she didn't know whether she was coming or going.

"One story which stands out in particular, was when she created a boyfriend to keep up with another student who had a boyfriend. The class knew she was lying so they asked her about her boyfriend, but she was unable to give too many details other than he was fighting in the Gulf War.

"The first girl started to get serious with her boyfriend. So, not to be outdone, the other girl said that she and her boyfriend were now engaged to be married. When we asked to see the engagement ring, she said that he was sending it. A couple of weeks later, sure enough, she had a ring. It wasn't much of a ring; it looked like a birthstone ring from a dollar store. But who am I to judge the depth of anyone's love? Now that she had a ring, the story was a little bit more believable.

"I had a meeting with the girl's mother so I asked her mother about the situation. 'Engaged!' she exclaimed. 'I bought that ring for her. She bugged me for two weeks about that stupid ring, and I finally gave in. If she's telling you she's engaged, she's full of it. I'll talk to her about it at home.'

"This did not help. The girl continued to tell us stories about her fiance and his adventures in the Gulf War. As we all know, the Gulf War was a short war. This was good for the country, but unfortunate for the girl. As the troops came home, the students in my class started asking the girl when her fiance was coming home. She told us how he was being moved from one part of Saudi Arabia to another and that the army still needed him.

"When the lie couldn't go on any longer, she came in crying one day – not to confess to the lie, but to tell us that her fiance had shot himself accidentally while cleaning his gun, and he was dead. That was the end to the boyfriend story, but not her lying."

We can also get so bogged down in saying what we think others want to hear that we forget to be honest. If we're honest with ourselves and others are honest with us, we can use that honesty to grow.

If someone asks your opinion, be honest. They asked, so that means that they want and probably respect your opinion. If you don't tell the truth, they can't make adjustments to themselves or whatever they asked your opinion about. Always remember not to let your honesty become cruel. There is enough hatefulness and cruelty in the world, so keep your honesty positive. If someone asks your opinion and you know that your opinion in its cruelest form will hurt or offend that person, find a way to be honest without blasting away at them. Don't hide behind a smokescreen of honesty as an excuse to put others down.

Beyond the lies we tell others are the lies which we tell ourselves. It seems as though there would be absolutely no advantage in lying to ourselves (and there's not), yet many of us do it all of the time.

Whether one creates low self-esteem by telling himself he's not as good as anyone else, or maybe he has a convoluted superior attitude because he's always telling himself that he's better than everyone else, it's unhappiness waiting to happen.

You're just you. That's all. Be the best you can be, but don't constantly compare yourself (favorably or unfavorably) to others around you. It can make you start thinking there's something wrong with you, and then all of sudden you're trying to pretend you're somebody you're not.

Since genuine conversations seem to be rare these days, it's quite refreshing to have one!

No man has a memory long enough to be a successful liar.

- Abraham Lincoln

You can't run from your lies.
They always catch up with you, and
they're bigger than you ever
intended for them to be!

23. Listen to people.

Listen to what people are saying when they talk to you. If you don't understand what someone is saying to you, ask him to repeat it. Listening can help prevent miscommunication, and anything we can do to prevent the chance of miscommunication will make us and everyone around us happier.

But beyond listening with our ears is listening with our other senses and our hearts. In the beginning stages of putting this book together, Ronnie's take on this concept was, "Don't just listen to the words, but how a person says the words. How you say something is just as important as what you say."

Terry, however, said, "Try to listen to what someone says, not how he says it."

Two totally different concepts it would seem! But after some careful consideration, we decided that both are important parts of listening to others.

Sometimes you know that a person is angry not at you but at a situation or maybe someone else. If such a person has occasion to speak to you, *please* just listen to the words he says and not the accompanying tone. It would definitely be nice if all of us had enough control over every aspect of how we communicate that our angry tone would only be directed at the appropriate situation or attitude, but unfortunately that's not the case. We can't expect everyone to always speak to us just exactly the way we want them to.

Now, on the other hand, if there aren't extenuating circumstances, then we can learn a lot about how someone is really feeling if we listen, not only to the words but how they're saying them. Watch their body language; it can speak volumes! Are they speaking loudly at an inappropriate time or perhaps softly and sadly. Content *and* tone are part of communication.

It's a package deal. If we really want to happily communicate with fewer misunderstandings and less hurt feelings, there are many things we'll consider as we have conversations with those around us.

Listening is an excellent communication skill.

24. Learn how to say no sometimes.

This is difficult when you're a "doer." A doer is a person who gets things done. People know a doer when they see one, and they will ask a doer to do things that need doing.

Doers get asked to do all kinds of things – mostly a lot of volunteer work. And while there is untold satisfaction in the giving of your time to help a cause for which you care, packing your schedule so full of committee meetings and fund raisers that you're exhausted is a happiness squelcher.

If you're one of those people who can't say "no," learn how fast because your happiness depends on it. Start with the small stuff and work your way up to the bigger things as you go. Don't feel guilty when you say no to someone's request for your time. Do it nicely, wish them success on their project and explain that you just can't add anything else to your schedule. You'll occasionally have to turn down a request for something that you'd really like to support (those are the tough ones), but teach yourself to do it.

Carefully choose the things that you deem *most important* to you, and do them well. Doing a bang-up job on one or two projects is far better than doing a mediocre job (or accomplishing nothing at all) on a dozen different things.

When you learn that it's okay to say no, you'll actually be

doing everyone, not just yourself, a service by not spreading your time too thin.

It's hard to be happy if you're overworked.

You probably shouldn't volunteer to make cookies for the bake sale if your kitchen is flooded.

25. Smile at everyone and be friendly.

This is a very important technique if you have any kind of job which requires you to work with people. It is also very important if you're pursuing happiness. A smile can work miracles. A smile can set the tone or mood of an encounter. A smile lays down the ground work for a pleasant exchange with another person. If you smile at people it's hard for them not to smile back.

When you smile, you feel better than when you frown or remain expressionless. There's lots of research to confirm this, but we know it by experience.

Terry's father is probably the overall, genuinely happiest person we know. He's *always* smiling, he's never down or depressed, and he's very friendly. He shakes hands with everyone he meets. Some of his friends started calling him "governor," because they jokingly asked him if was running for office.

He's an encourager and a complimenter. He tells kids that they're "good helpers," checks on people when they're sick, and reminds everyone to have a good day. People can't help but smile when they talk to him.

One time he saw a dollar bill which had been folded into a "bow tie" shape. He thought it was such a clever idea that he figured out how to do it himself, and now he gives dollar bill bow ties to people on special occasions: birthdays, graduations, accomplishments of any kind.

He even made up a little poem to go along with the dollar. It goes like this:

Though he's folded and badly bent,
You're not broke, if he's not spent.

At 78 years old, he's seen a lot of sadness, but he hasn't chosen to let that become his focus in life. His goal is to meet people with a smile and walk away with a new friend.

26. Presentation is usually 99% of acceptance.

Do you find that you're often frustrated and unhappy because it seems as though you have good ideas, but everybody else dismisses them immediately? Do you have important things to say, but nobody ever listens? Do you try to sell things and meet with continual rejection? You're certain you could change the world if only you could convince others to do what you suggest!

This is not a book about getting others to do what you want them to do, and while getting your way should not be a requirement for happiness, you'll find that as your attitude about life in general improves, you will have more and more positive thoughts and good ideas that really will better your life and the lives of others. But if those around you only remember the old, unhappy you who never had any good ideas, they may not want to listen to what you have to say.

How you say something is just as important as what you say. Think about how you address others. Do you order people around or do you *ask* people to do things? Do you grunt a hello or do you look at people and say hello like you mean it? If you are an orderer or a grunter, you may be adding to your unhappiness by presenting yourself as an unhappy person. If you present yourself in a happy way, you will find that it's easier to be happy.

This concept goes beyond daily communication; it also works with presenting projects and new ideas. If we go into a situation like gang busters, we can expect to be treated like gang busters. We may have good ideas, but we can turn people off by being too overbearing, (*or* too meek). It may not seem right, but people judge others by how they speak and present themselves.

It's frustrating when people have trouble understanding your ideas. If others are not accepting what you have to say, maybe you should look into changing the way you convey your thoughts. (You may also need to take a closer look at what you're trying to convey to make sure it really is appropriate to the situation.)

This isn't a *scientific* fact, but if you'll stop and notice most situations around you, you'll discover that presentation is probably 99% of acceptance.

One good example of this is people (often children) sent out by various organizations (school groups, for example), who wish to raise money by selling things (usually candy bars, it would seem). Terry has had them walk right in the front door of her business, and rather timidly say, "You wouldn't want to buy a candy bar, would you?"

"No. I wouldn't. But thanks anyway," is her reply.

Don't set yourself up for failure by being negative. Whether you're selling a product, a service or an idea, start by believing in what you're doing. Take on a positive attitude about it and assume that others will also see it in a good light if they know all the facts. Don't present yourself arrogantly, but do make your presentation confidently.

Here's an example of a sales pitch that would probably sell us an over-priced candy bar almost every time:

A smiling youngster politely says, "Hi, my name is Kelly. I'm selling candy bars to help my school buy a new computer. I have two different kinds, both of them are really good, and they only cost a dollar each. Would you like to buy one?"

Well sure! In fact, we might even buy two. It's the same product rejected in the first example, the only difference is in the presentation.

Apply the same principles in presenting your ideas at work or in other groups. Speak up, smile, be polite and tell all the reasons why your plan is wonderful.

We shouldn't be conniving and manipulative, but we can be observant – the more we know about the person or group we're dealing with, the more we can mold our presentation so they'll embrace it. We can head off disappointments by knowing the part of our plan that will be most easily accepted and presenting that part first, de-emphasizing anything that might be controversial or drastic.

A little planning and forethought into what you'll actually say (and *how* you'll say it) in presenting an idea will be a tremendous help in achieving acceptance.

27. Know-it-alls are annoying.

Monopolizing conversations by constantly insisting on being right and being the sole provider of what you consider to be useful information is a good way to insure that you will only have conversations with yourself! And while there's nothing wrong with talking to yourself, it's a real shame when you're forced to do it because you're the only one who will listen!

Those who think they know everything probably won't have many friends because, as a general rule, know-it-alls are pretty selfish people, always desiring to be the one who is heard to the exclusion of everyone else. (Not a quality we seek in our friends.)

Maybe people think it makes them happy to be at the center of attention, but what they don't realize is how much they're missing out on by not letting others contribute to conversations. Know-it-alls never really learn anything new, and that's not a very satisfying way to live.

Try to back off of sharing everything you know when you're talking to someone else. (Reserve some of that fount of knowledge for future conversations.) Don't keep bringing the focus back to you and what you want to talk about. Ask questions and don't automatically disagree with the answers!

We should strive to let others be heard, and let ourselves be often silent.

Know-it-alls often dine alone.

28. Seek advice from those made wise by experience, but give advice sparingly.

Getting (or giving) good advice makes a person happy. Getting (or giving) bad advice makes us unhappy. Advice is a dangerous thing among friends. While good advice reinforces friendships, bad advice can ruin a friendship.

If you're having a problem, and you're looking for advice in the matter from a friend or acquaintance, you're probably better off to seek out someone who has been through a similar situation. They'll be able to give you an insight about what they did which helped them get through it, and what they may have wished they had done differently.

Unless someone is just naturally good at giving advice (a rare talent), maybe you shouldn't ask them to give you counsel if they haven't experienced a problem similar to yours. Of the people who you hang around with the most, you should be able to tell by their track records who gives good advice and who doesn't. Here's some advice about advice: if someone always advises you to do things which turn out to be bad or wrong, don't seek advice from that person! Continue to be his friend, but filter what he tells you.

Remember that someone who is 60 years old (unless he's made stupid mistakes his entire life!) will generally give better advice than someone who is 20 years old, simply because he has lived longer and experienced more things. Don't automatically dismiss advice from young people, but do consider it carefully.

In a similar vein, give advice sparingly. Important, life-changing decisions are made every day based on advice, so we should all give careful thought to what we tell other people they should or shouldn't do. We shouldn't try to be something we're not, and if we don't know the answer to a person's problem, it's best to honestly tell them so. We shouldn't have to feel compelled to say something, when we don't really know what we're talking about.

It's a sad thing to see a person follow someone's counsel into disaster. Neither party is happy when that happens.

29. Be a mentor.

We've all heard that you can't put a price tag on experience, and it's true. We should all be willing to help someone who is just starting out in an area about which we're already familiar. Let's not hoard our knowledge; let's share it.

Many of us have benefitted from someone who gave us a hand when we were just starting out in a new venture, and many more of us have wished that someone would have been willing to share their expertise with us.

If you're in a position of leadership or authority, you'll discover that the best way to get good results from those around you is to empower them. Help them to grow and move ahead. Never feel threatened when you see others advancing. Be happy for them, and don't try to squelch them in any way.

One of the greatest sources of happiness in your own life can be seeing others around you become successful, in part, because you have taken the time to be a positive influence on their lives. Become an encourager. Exhort others to set goals and help them achieve more and better things. If you use your experience to help enrich others' lives, you will find that you become enriched and happier.

We must tread lightly in this area, however. We shouldn't be overbearing, forcing our opinions on those who don't really want our suggestions. Nobody likes to be ordered around and told what to do. We must find ways to offer suggestions and not make commandments. It is, after all, not *our* life. It is someone else's life we're talking about here, and they must ultimately choose their own road.

"My fifth grade teacher, Mr. Bryan, was one of the mentors in my life," recalls Terry. "And I doubt if he even has an idea how much he helped direct the course I've taken in life.

"Growing up in a rural area of the Ozarks, I had limited access to art instruction, and I was very interested in drawing and painting, the only forms of artistic expression with which I was familiar.

"Mr. Bryan was an artist who also happened to be an elementary school teacher. He took the job of fifth grade teacher at my school the year I entered fifth grade, and my life was almost immediately changed for the better. He incorporated art into his regular classroom curriculum and began teaching us basic things about form and design and color. And when our school had open house, we displayed our artwork on the wall for our parents to see. Mr. Bryan praised my work and told my mom and dad that I was a very good artist.

"He was such an encourager to me that from then on, art and design became a significant part of what I pursued. It has continued to be not only a source of enjoyment in my life, but it has in some way been related to every job I've ever had.

"He only taught at my school for a couple of years, then he moved back to his home in Kansas, and I've never seen him again. But Mr. Bryan, if you ever have occasion to read this, I want to thank you and tell you that you had a tremendous impact on the life of one little fifth grade girl in the Ozarks."

*Whatever is your specialty –
be sure to share your expertise!*

30. It's okay to say "I don't know."

Many of us have trouble admitting that we don't have all of the answers. When someone asks us a question, we'd rather make up something instead of saying we don't know.

We're not born knowing everything, and, in fact, *no one* knows *everything*. We've had to learn from the time we were born until now. We may not remember, but there was a time when we couldn't talk or read or do anything for ourselves!

We all learn things every day; we never stop learning. By saying "I don't know," we can open ourselves up to new experiences and more knowledge, which is almost always a good thing.

Additionally, we don't appear to be stupid or lacking in authority for honestly saying, "I don't know." The main reason this relates to our own state of happiness is that it can keep us from looking foolish when it's discovered (and it *will be* discovered) that we haven't really got a clue whether what we're saying is accurate or not.

Terry's husband, Allen, his brother and a friend like to take "road trips" from time to time. Usually they're going somewhere for a specific, important reason (like attending a car show), but they've discovered that getting there is more than half the fun because they have so many misadventures along the way.

One thing that happens every trip is that they get lost at least once. And they get lost because whoever is driving won't admit he doesn't know where he's going. He would much rather drive an hour out of the way than ask for directions. To him, driving aimlessly is better than saying, "I don't know where I'm going."

This would be a better example for our point if these guys didn't actually *enjoy* getting lost. (In fact, they expect it now and look forward to it every trip.) However, most people don't share their enthusiasm for such things and will acknowledge that it's better to ask for directions than waste a lot of travel time being lost.

A man should never be ashamed to own he has been in the wrong, which is but saying in other words, that he is wiser today than he was yesterday. - Alexander Pope

31. Spreading rumors is a bad habit.

There's no way to justify saying bad or questionable things about a person behind his or her back. It is not communicating or "sharing." It's just a bad idea.

Rumors can be about anything or anybody. The person telling the rumor may even have good intentions, but rumors aren't good for anybody.

One time there was a rumor going around at the school where Ronnie worked that a certain restaurant in town was closed down because someone there had hepatitis A. Ronnie knew his parents ate there often so he called home to tell his mother the distressing news. After he told her the story, his mother said, "Last week when we were eating there our hostess told us not to come in to eat next week because they were going to be closed for vacation."

Ronnie realized that the news he had heard was just a rumor. Even though Ronnie had good intentions, he had been a victim of the rumor mill.

Rumors can get started so easily. Ronnie had a student make a comment after another student wouldn't drink after her. She said, "Don't worry, I don't have AIDS." While Ronnie's para-educator was scolding the student for using the word AIDS as if it were nothing more serious than "cooties," another student, hearing the end of the conversation asked, "Who has AIDS?" If Ronnie hadn't stopped the rumor in its tracks, who knows how the story would have ended.

Even when people are repeating the truth, it can get turned around. We're sure everyone has played the "Rumor" game where a group of people sit in a circle and then one person whispers a phrase to the person next to him, and it's repeated until the phrase has gone around the circle. The message at the end is seldom exactly the same as it was when it started.

If we can't manage to say something good about someone, we shouldn't say anything at all. If we live by this motto, we'll become happier because we're not saying negative things.

Negative thoughts lead to negative feelings, and negative feelings make it harder to be happy. If you have a problem with something that someone is doing, talk about it *to them*. There's no reason to discuss it with anyone else; it simply doesn't accomplish anything positive. If you talk to other people about it, the person you have the problem with won't know there's a problem. If he doesn't know there is a problem, then he can't make adjustments or restitutions. By discussing it with the person whom you have a problem with, instead of gossiping to others, you will help yourself and others be happier. (Resolving conflict makes everyone happy!)

Once we start talking about people and their shortcomings, all those insulting comments just begin to roll off our tongues so easily that before long, we don't even realize we're doing it. We assassinate someone's character with little or no evidence and don't even blink when we're saying it.

"Well, I heard she . . ."

How many conversations are we involved in which begin with that comment and end with something negative? We should never start a conversation with that phrase, nor participate in one that begins with that phrase unless we're *praising* someone.

Additionally, if we spread rumors, we will lose friends. The only friends we'll have are other gossip mongers, and they make terrible friends because everything we tell them (about ourselves or others) they'll repeat to someone else!

When we hear an unsavory bit of information about someone, we should stifle the desire to repeat it. We *can* develop self-control, especially in the area of gossip. By doing so, we can avoid the feelings of guilt which often come with knowing we've been less than we could have been if we had refrained from saying hurtful things.

32. Yelling should be reserved for life-threatening situations and other real emergencies.

We're curious about people who yell a lot. Why do they do it? Are they always angry? Do they think they can't be heard without raising their voices? Do they like to draw attention to themselves? Maybe they're just unhappy, and they'd like to make sure everyone else is also miserable, because it is definitely agonizing to be around someone who yells all of the time.

When an individual goes around yelling about everything and to everybody, nobody knows when he's serious. On the other hand, if we save the yelling for those times when we really need to get a point across, people will be more likely to listen. Ronnie notes that living by this motto has helped him in emergencies. He relates a story about a classroom situation:

"My para-educator was in my room watching the class. I was outside my classroom door talking to a student about his work and behavior. I heard a commotion coming from the classroom. I opened up the door and there was one of my students (a senior girl) holding a knife on a freshman boy. I yelled the girl's name. She looked at me. I made eye contact with her and yelled her name again. Then I said, *'Put away the knife and come out here, NOW!'* I could tell she was shocked that I yelled at her because I'd never done it before. It seemed to break her out of her trance. She dropped the knife and walked over to me."

If Ronnie had been a yeller and yelled at his students all of the time, would he have made the same impact? We believe not. His approach to the situation may have saved the life of a student.

Please don't yell. It creates a very unpleasant environment. There is no reason for it unless you need to alert others to impending danger, or, like Ronnie in the example above, you need to make a drastic point. Plus, the ones being yelled at never know whether they're doing anything right. If you're a yeller, stop and take a look at why and when you're yelling. When you decide to stop, not only will everyone around you appreciate a rest for their ears, but a *kinder, gentler* you will be a *happier* you.

33. Choose your battles carefully.

If a person fights everybody on every issue, he accomplishes two things: he'll likely kill himself trying, and like "the boy who cried wolf," he'll lose his credibility. Others will soon start ignoring him. People will think he's merely a troublemaker instead of someone who is standing up for his beliefs.

Some things are definitely worth holding our ground and not backing down in the face of opposition. Other things aren't worth the effort.

Terry remembers a couple of years ago being involved in an organization which needed to purchase new tables. The tables were to be used occasionally in a large room for group meals.

An unexpected controversy broke out when one person suggested that round tables would enable more people to be seated at one time than an equal number of standard, rectangular, folding tables. The group took sides on the matter – theories were advanced, sketches of the room were produced – and the controversy continued over the course of the next several weeks and months, even though the total seating capacity would not have been affected by more than a half-dozen people one way or the other.

The discussion managed to be good-natured in tone (most of the time), but the eventual outcome was that *no* new tables, round or rectangular, were ever purchased! An ill-chosen battle turned out to be quite counter-productive because every time the group has a get-together there are still a lot of people sitting around on folding chairs, balancing paper plates on their knees because there isn't enough table space to go around. (Imagine that same organization, a few months later, trying to decide on new carpet!)

Don't seek out controversy by always taking a stand on every issue that comes along. Choose things which are truly important to you and devote some of your time and energy to endorsing those things. And promote with a positive message, not negative, annoying ones. You've probably heard that old saying that you catch more flies with honey than vinegar, so don't think you'll win many people over with a yelling, screaming, in-your-face attitude. That kind of behavior is very tiresome and turns many potential supporters of a cause off before they ever really hear the message.

Championing a cause will surely bring a person happiness. Becoming a public nuisance with a crusade over every minor issue will not win anyone many friends.

In a similar vein, one should learn when to be assertive and when not to be assertive. If a person's not careful, he may be seen as a shrew and not as someone supporting a worthy cause.

Standing up for what we believe is an important factor in being happy, but choosing our battles carefully is also necessary.

*Fighting everyone all of the time
often has unpleasant
consequences.*

34. Don't threaten unless you mean to carry out the threat.

Hey, if we don't have any intention of carrying through on something, let's save our time and don't even initiate it. This is especially true with threats and is excellent advice for parents and others who work with children.

Too many families don't really communicate. Oh, they may talk *at* each other and do lots of yelling, but everyone is pretty unhappy because the kids get their way all of the time, and the parents don't seem to have any control. They usually lose control right at the point when they start making idle threats.

"If you don't stop that begging, I'm never bringing you to Toyland again!" (Oh, really? We don't believe it for a minute, and the kids don't either.)

Halfway to the Grand Canyon on a family vacation, "You stop pestering your sister, or we'll turn this car around right now and go home!" (One of our favorite idle threats.)

That stuff sounds mostly like sitcom fodder, but those are the things you hear in so many households (and sometimes school rooms, too) on a daily basis. Parents (and teachers) who make threats without carrying them out should just keep quiet right from the start. We should say what we mean and mean what we say.

This may hurt sometimes because we threaten something that we wish we hadn't. But as threateners, we have to think about the threat *before* we make it. Making threats and then not carrying through is the sort of thing that leads to frustration for everyone, not to a lot of peace and happiness. Parents are not helping anyone – not the child, not themselves – by this behavior.

Threats should be kept to a minimum, but if we make them, we should be sure that they are reasonable threats and that we do intend to carry them out.

35. Try to avoid developing the habit of automatically saying either "yes" or "no" to requests.

This really should apply to everyone who makes a request of us, but it is particularly important for parents to keep this in mind when dealing with their children.

When a child makes a request, a parent shouldn't routinely answer without first considering the request. This applies especially to saying "no!" right away. What the child is asking may actually be something quite reasonable. When the parent has to re-consider, after having said "no" to start with, credibility and consistency suffer.

When a person listens to each request and takes a moment to consider the reason behind the request, it may be discovered that the request is reasonable and has merit, and there is really no cause to say no.

We should also not be in the habit of always saying "yes" to our children. There are many unpleasant people in the world who were accustomed to getting everything they asked for as children. Very often kids ask for things they don't really need, things inappropriate for them or even potentially dangerous to them. It's certainly okay to say no sometimes (mandatory, actually). Just don't do it all of the time.

Stopping to consider individual requests based on their merit is a good way to develop good communication with your child (and others). It will help you become a better listener, and listening carefully to your child can sometimes cue you in to some problems he or she may be having. In the long run, you will be a happier person when you listen to your children.

Hang out with your kids once in a while and listen to what they have to say.

36. When confronting someone about a situation, concentrate on the behaviors with which you don't agree, not on the person.

If you do this, your confrontation will become an attack on the behavior and not an attack on the person. Launching a verbal attack on anyone is not a step in the direction of happiness.

Once someone feels he's being attacked, it becomes impossible to have an open conversation. Some will be put on the defensive, and others won't even discuss the issue. Once this occurs, you won't be able to discuss the behavior you were wanting to talk about, and the other person's feelings may be hurt. Either can make happiness seem that much further away.

Ronnie does this in his class for students with behavior disorders. He often has students who are "neat" people, but they have unacceptable behavior. When Ronnie confronts a student about a behavior, he has to focus on the *behavior* that is inappropriate and not on the student. He tells the student, "Hey, you're a neat kid. I like you [only if it's truly the way he feels], but I don't like the way you hit that other student. You could have really hurt him, and there are other ways to deal with problems."

The same applies to our dealing with others, and especially parents dealing with children. If you catch your child smoking, for example, don't call him stupid (this attacks the child). Instead, tell him that you love him, and you don't want him to die of a disease caused by cigarettes (this attacks the behavior).

If we put others down (especially children), we can cause real and lasting damage to their self-esteem and cause the behavior, which we were trying to improve, to actually get worse.

"Godzilla, you're a really great monster, but eating that car will give you indigestion, and it might also cause your insurance rates to increase."

37. Communicate with yourself.

One common cause of unhappiness is agonizing over a decision, especially when it comes to confrontations and conflicts. "Should I or shouldn't I approach her with this problem? Are we even having a problem? Should I tell him what I really think? Maybe I just need to give her a piece of my mind!" (Should we ever give anyone a piece of our minds? No, we shouldn't. You see, no matter how smart we are, none of us have any to spare for those purposes!)

When we're having trouble deciding if we should do something or say something to someone, let's ask ourselves, "Why am I doing this? What is the purpose of the task or the question? *What is my motivation?*"

We've both used this test for decision-making on numerous occasions. Terry and her husband applied this criteria in making a particularly difficult decision about leaving the church where they had been members for many years.

"When Allen and I felt we needed to move on from the only church we had ever attended in the 16 years we had been married, it was not an easy decision for us.

"We knew that many people in the church might misunderstand our actions and be upset or hurt by our leaving, and we didn't want that to happen. But we finally decided that even though it might appear to some that we were leaving for the wrong reasons, we had carefully examined our motivation and were comfortable with our reasons and our decision. We couldn't let the fear of what others might say cloud our thinking on the matter.

"It was still a difficult thing to do, but we achieved a sense of peace about the situation which has allowed us to move on without feelings of guilt and distress."

When we truthfully examine our motivations for making decisions, we usually don't have any doubts as to whether we should do or say a particular thing.

38. Be patient when communicating with others.

Communication is not always easy. Sometimes people don't understand the information you are communicating to them. Realize that others have different backgrounds and experiences on which to base the information you are communicating.

When we communicate, we draw on our past experiences to understand information that is presented to us. Certain words may trigger certain images or feelings. These feelings and images may be the complete opposite of what you think of when you hear the exact same words. For example, we're going to give you a word. Read the word and think about it. Don't read any further until you have a clear image of the word in your head. Are you ready? The word is *dog*. Think about it for a moment and visualize a dog. . . .

What did you see? Did you imagine a Great Dane or a Chihuahua? Maybe you imagined a Dalmatian (Terry's personal favorite) or any of the hundreds of other breeds of dogs. If we were trying to communicate the idea of having a dog sit in the lap of a model, and you thought of a Great Dane, you may think it was a terrible idea, or comical at best.

That was an easy word. It's a concrete word that most of us pick up by the age of two. Think of a more complicated, abstract word like . . . *happy*. We all have different images of and feelings about happiness, and we all communicate differently. We bring different information to the table of communication. Remember when you communicate with others that they may not understand because of their different experiences in life. If you remember this, you may not be so easily frustrated by their seeming lack of understanding, and you'll have a better chance of communicating your ideas.

An assortment of happy dogs.

BE CAREFUL

Be careful of your thoughts
For your thoughts become your words.

Be careful of your words
For your words become your actions.

Be careful of your actions
For your actions become your habits.

Be careful of your habits
For your habits become your character.

Be careful of your character
For your character becomes your destiny.

- author unknown

Chapter Three

Deal Well with People and Situations

We all encounter difficult people and trying circumstances as we live each day, but it's not what happens to us in life that really matters.

> *What really*
> > *matters is how*
> > > *we react to what*
> > > > *happens to us . . .*

39. Life is what YOU make it.

We are all in charge of making the decisions which affect our happiness and the outcome of our lives. The actions of others should not affect our happiness in a negative way. We must decide that we will be happy no matter what others around us are doing (or not doing).

During his college years, Ronnie encountered a man who could have definitely had a permanent negative impact on his life if Ronnie had chosen to allow it. We'll call this man "Dr. Doe"; he was the chairman of the Physical Education Department where Ronnie attended college. Ronnie tells the story:

"I have always been overweight, but I'm proud of the fact that I never let my weight stop me from doing what I wanted to do. So when I decided that I wanted to take a couple of P.E. classes in college, I did it. The teachers were great; I loved both of them (Mrs. Albright, my swimming teacher, and Dr. Adams, my physical conditioning teacher).

"After being inspired by teachers like that, I decided I wanted to be a P.E. major. To be a P.E. major, a student has to go through a screening process. The screening committee looks at grades, ACT score, and overall personality. I was a little nervous about going before the committee, but I also knew I had the grades and ACT score which I needed, and I had always been known as the 'nice guy' so I figured that this was just a formality.

"I was escorted to a room where the screening committee was waiting for me. This was my first encounter with Dr. Doe – there he sat along with Dr. Adams, Mrs. Albright and other instructors from the P.E. Department. As Dr. Doe looked at my grades and my application, I could sense an uneasiness about him. He wanted to say something, but he didn't know how to say it. After an uncomfortable silence, he said, 'Well, looking at the A's you have received in your P.E. classes at college . . . and those are not easy classes . . . it would seem . . . that . . . well . . .'

"Dr. Adams interrupted, smiling, 'What he's trying to say Ronnie, is you move your mass well.'

"Knowing Dr. Adams's sense of humor, I said, 'Thank you. I take pride in the way I move my mass.'

"We all laughed except for Dr. Doe who didn't want to let it go at that; he wanted to talk about my weight. (I didn't know it at the time, but Dr. Doe was considering not letting me be a P.E. major because of my weight.)

"Dr. Adams's warped sense of humor (which I had gotten accustomed to and learned to enjoy in his class) helped me get through the first encounter with Dr. Doe.

"The next time I had a major encounter with him was my senior year. He called a meeting with Mrs. Albright (my advisor), another student who was also overweight, and me. In this meeting, he told us that he was ashamed of us, we were an embarrassment to the Department, we would never get jobs as physical educators, and he was considering not letting us graduate because we were overweight.

"This man did manage to make my senior year miserable. I was worried about whether or not I was going to graduate. I asked myself if I should try to find a different major, but I knew I was only one semester away from student teaching and graduation. I also knew I did not have the time or the money to change majors. With help from Mrs. Albright, Dr. Adams and a few others, we both made it through our senior year and graduated.

"Dr. Doe would have settled for nothing less that ruining my entire life if I would have let him, but I wouldn't give his attitude that kind of power over me. Today, my self-esteem is good, and I've decided that my memory of his actions will never negatively affect me again."

People, by nature, do things which disappoint. Unlike Dr. Doe, many people really do have good intentions, but even at that, friends, family and associates will sometimes let us down.

We can't blame our unhappiness on those around us; life just isn't designed to be that way. Each of us must take responsibility for our actions and for our own happiness. We must not dwell on the unkind, sometimes even cruel and heartless, comments that are thrown about every day. There is no pleasure to be derived from placing emphasis on the negative things of life.

You and only you are in charge of your life and how you deal with people and situations. If you're the type of person who lets the moods of those around you affect your own mood, you're going to live a yo-yo life. Decide that you are the one who will control what mood you will be in. You'll find that others will follow you. It's harder to be unhappy when you're with someone who's happy. If you take charge of your happiness, no matter who or what you must deal with, you will be happier because *you decide to be happy.*

Put on your armor just like a coat of wax on a car. Have you ever noticed how water turns into tiny beads and just rolls right off a freshly-waxed automobile? Let the unhappy, bad things in life have the same effect on you.

You simply cannot depend on others for your own happiness.

Happiness grows at our own fireside and is not to be picked in a stranger's garden.

- Douglas Jerrold

Take charge of your own happiness.

40. Try to find the good in everyone and every situation.

If we look hard enough, even the very worst things and people that we encounter have some goodness in them. And the very worst is not what we encounter on an everyday basis – usually, we'll just meet up with average situations and people, and certainly, there is a lot of good to be found in average things!

This "looking for a silver lining in every cloud" attitude is one which will bring you a great deal of happiness. There are few people who are absolutely evil, and no situation is totally bad. Someone who seems to be doing everything for the wrong reasons, from your point of view, may actually have some very good reasons for his actions. If you can find out what those reasons are, it will help you understand that person and understand why he does what he does. (But even if you don't know the reason someone behaves in a certain way, you shouldn't *make assumptions* about his behavior.)

We know a man who is one of the happiest people we've met. He doesn't speak poorly of others, even the ones he doesn't really like (and there aren't very many of those). He smiles a lot and has a good time. He believes that everything will turn out okay in the end.

His wife, on the other hand, can't really find too much to be happy about. One time, she had not been feeling well, and she went to the doctor. He found some kind of small growth which he determined needed to be removed. She was immediately distraught and decided she was going to die.

"I just *know* it's cancer," she said.

Her husband reminded her that no diagnosis had been made, and that it was quite likely just a benign cyst. He also mentioned that even in the event it might be cancer, it was caught early enough that the surgery would remove it, and then, if needed, chemotherapy treatments would ensure that any remaining cells would be completely destroyed.

"I'm sure it's cancer. But it probably doesn't matter because I know I'll die when they do the surgery to take it out anyway," she said.

"It's routine surgery, and there's no reason to believe you're going to die," he reminded her.

"What will you and the kids do without me?" she asked.

"We'll be fine no matter what, but we're not going to have to worry about doing without you. You're going to be *fine*!"

"Oh, what's going to happen when I die?" she wailed.

Exasperated, but still positive, he said, "Then you'll go to Heaven, and what can be wrong with *that*?!"

(His faith prevailed in this situation. Her tumor was benign, and there were no complications from the surgery.)

Most of our day to day life is not so dramatic as contemplating serious disease or illness, but the level of our daily happiness is determined by how we approach even the smallest disturbances which we encounter.

Find the good things and build on them. Discard the bad.

Well . . . at least there aren't any alligators.

41. Give others the benefit of the doubt.

If we hear something negative about someone, or even if we witness that person doing something which appears to be questionable to us, we shouldn't automatically assume the worst. Most of the time, we don't have all of the facts, and we can quickly jump to the wrong conclusion. Friendships can be damaged or destroyed because of simple misunderstandings based on incomplete information.

Always give others the benefit of the doubt. If you think someone has done something wrong or hurtful to you, find out the truth before you act on your feelings. Giving others the benefit of the doubt before you react to their actions is the only way to go when dealing with people. This will help clear up any misunderstandings before they occur. It's easier to be happy if you react to the truth instead of reacting to what you *think* the truth might be.

Don't concentrate on the motives of others. Constantly thinking that they are trying to make you unhappy will indeed have just that effect.

Hasty judgments are dangerous. If you're in the habit of making snap decisions about people (or things or choices in your life), please stop and become a more thoughtful person.

Remember, no matter what you see a person doing, he may have a perfectly logical explanation for his behavior.

42. Give credit where credit is due.

We shouldn't be glory hogs! Not only should we make sure we never take credit for accomplishments that are not our own, we must always actively give others credit for their achievements.

Unless you've become calloused by years of taking the recognition which others deserve, you'll find yourself to be very unhappy with feelings of guilt when you take credit that is not yours for the taking. It's not fair to the person who deserved the credit because you have been a thief; you have actually stolen something which rightfully belongs to another.

Put away the desire to get all the pats on the back and share the limelight with those around you. You should never look around at what others are accomplishing and jealously decide you must be better than they are. There are no winners in one-upmanship games.

To borrow a catch-phrase which was especially popular in the 1980s, be a "team player." Work for and work with those around you, seeking common ground and looking toward the same goals. There is strength in numbers and if you are lucky enough to be on a team, embrace the opportunity. Participate on the team and do your share.

The success of a team is your success. Always feeling the need to shine individually is a selfish and ultimately unfulfilling way to live.

Behind every good boss is a really great secretary.

43. Know that, in general, people are not out to get you.

Not only are people not out to get us, but mostly, they don't even care the least about what we're doing! They're so busy living their own lives they don't want to take time out to concentrate on how to make us miserable. (Granted, many of them are quite good at doing that without even trying, but most of the time they don't do it intentionally.)

It's easy to get caught up in the feeling that everybody is out to get you. This feeling is magnified on days when nothing seems to be going right. But if you sit back and think about it rationally, you will realize that it's not true. As a matter of fact, why not believe that people are there to *help* one another? Once you decide that, take the information and live each day as a member of a giant society of helpers.

Okay, that sounds a little corny, but it's a lot better than thinking that everyone is out to get you and living your life beat down and defeated. If you believe in the idea of being part of a whole society of helpers, it will be easier for you to live each day happily.

Also remember that we should all try not to take things so personally. Those around us are prone to make offhanded comments that we think are directed at us, but the world does not revolve around any individual. We shouldn't put ourselves in the center of attention by reading too much into what people say.

It's also a waste of valuable time being paranoid and constantly trying to figure out the ulterior motives of other people. Rarely are any of us average folks ever the targets of conspiracies.

Seeking out mysterious conspiracies and plots to get you is a waste of time.

44. Respect everyone.

We should never put ourselves or anyone else down. Instead, we should allow a genuine admiration for the good qualities of others to flow out of us. There are enough negative things in this world without adding to the stack. This includes speaking negatively about others and ourselves. Name-calling and condescending attitudes have no place in a happy life.

Let's be polite. When we're listening to someone, we should be courteous enough to give them our full attention. Take into consideration the feelings of others and never intentionally say hurtful things.

Always be gracious and don't make inappropriate comments.

Have a special reverence for senior citizens, and look to their experience as a guiding light.

Never attempt to steal another's dignity. Be a protector of people. Hold them up. Build them up. Be respectful.

Do nothing from selfishness or empty conceit, but with humility of mind let each of you regard one another as more important than himself; do not merely look out for your own personal interests, but also for the interests of others.

PHILIPPIANS 2:3-4
NASB
Thomas Nelson Publishers
©1977 The Lockman Foundation

45. Hate serves no useful purpose.

As powerful as love is to the breaking down of barriers, hate is also powerful in the building of barriers. Hate is a strong and destructive force, and yet, many of us use the word quite casually.

"I hate broccoli."

"I hate going to Aunt Mary's house."

"I hate him."

We should be careful not to attach such strong emotions to things which we don't like or simply don't care to do. We can convince ourselves of all kinds of things when we continually say something over and over again. We can truly come to hate things and people, and that is never a good idea.

We may not like being around someone because of his or her behavior, but we should not hate that person. There is enough hate in the world as it is without adding some more to it, but at the same time it's asking too much of anyone to *like* everybody. There are too many personalities, and we're bound to find some we don't care for. But just because we don't *like* someone, we mustn't hate them!

We all have been in situations where we had to deal with someone we preferred not to, but we went ahead and did it for the greater good. That's a good lesson for us all. It helps things run more smoothly, and it will make us better appreciate the people we do enjoy being around. Sometimes we will have to be around people we don't like, but if we want to be happy, we must not hate them.

And if you find yourself on the receiving end of hate, don't return that hate with more hate. Hate breeds hate, and it is a negative attitude that makes it impossible to be happy. Breaking cycles of hostility is crucial in building and maintaining a happy, healthy lifestyle and doing your part to contribute to a better society.

Learn to love your fellow man.

The hatred we bear our enemies injures their happiness less than our own.
　　　　　　　　　　　　　　　　- J. Petit-Senn

46. Break cycles of prejudice and bigotry.

Being narrow-minded is not an ingredient in the recipe for happiness – not even a pinch of it is called for!

How many times can it be said that a person's appearance, skin color, religion, social standing or any other factor in which he may be different from us should never determine what we think about that person. See each person as a person. Concentrate on your similarities and appreciate your differences.

Even those who live their lives in a way to which we fundamentally object, should not be cast aside as persons, and they should not be condemned or ridiculed. If we truly believe their behavior is destructive, we should care enough about them to be a friend and have a positive influence on them. We should live our lives as an example to them.

While we were writing this book, a story on the news caught our attention. At a Ku Klux Klan rally, a group of people gathered to demonstrate their disapproval of the Klan's agenda.

During the course of the demonstration, both groups began yelling at each other. A man from the KKK group fell in amongst the anti-Klan protesters who started kicking and beating him. A young black woman placed herself between the man and the angry mob, using her body as a shield to protect him while pleading with the others to stop beating him. They did stop, and the man was allowed to return to his group.

This young woman risked her own life to save a man who hated her race. She realized that actions speak louder than words and that answering hate with more hate can accomplish nothing positive. She was willing to take the first step in breaking the cycle of prejudice, fear, and resentment.

Let us hope the man whose life she saved, and all of those who witnessed her act of bravery, will take the next step.

Additionally, we all must remember that, ultimately, we are only responsible for ourselves. Everyone must choose his own path. Whether or not your path leads to happiness, even if you've been on the receiving end of hate, is entirely up to you.

47. Be forgiving.

A true happiness blocker is harboring unforgiveness. Unforgiveness leads to resentment and bitterness and all kinds of unpleasantness. In fact, we're convinced that unforgiveness causes more unhappiness than almost anything else.

Self-centeredness makes us become offended over the least little infringement, and an unforgiving attitude makes that offense grow over time until it turns into a huge violation of our rights. We must not allow that to happen, so we can't waste our time dwelling on the past. People are going to make mistakes; there's no getting around that fact. We have to get over it, and get on with our lives and the business of being happy.

Ronnie tells a story of forgiveness:

"I'm a hunter and landowner, and I'm against poaching and road hunting. One morning during deer season, my brother was getting ready to go to work. As he was going out the door of his home, he saw a truck go past his house and a few seconds later he heard a gun shot. He immediately got into his truck and drove in the direction of the shot.

"As he got closer to where the shot had come from, he could see the truck that had just gone by his house parked on the side of the road. He then looked into the woods and saw a man dressed in orange dragging a deer from our property.

"My brother asked the man some questions, and after a lengthy conversation, the man asked my brother if he wanted the deer. My brother replied by saying, 'No, if I had wanted the deer, I would have shot the deer.'

"We decided not to turn the road hunter in to the Conservation Department, but his actions continued to aggravate me. Road hunting is against the law for a very good reason. Someone can be **killed** when a person shoots into the woods. I could have been hunting, or worse, someone in my family could have been hunting in those woods. I wanted to turn the guy in or call him up and give him a piece of my mind or make him give the meat to a homeless shelter – something, anything to make this guy pay for his sins.

"I let it eat at me day and night until it grew into rage, and I finally realized that it was making me miserable. I was allowing this man and his actions to make me unhappy. I decided I had to forgive him and go on. It was not my place to make him pay for his wrong doings. I do believe he will have to pay for his actions, but it was not meant for me to be the judge and the jury.

"After I forgave him for his trespasses against me and my family, I was much happier."

There is another side to forgiving that people often like to claim has nothing to do with it, and that's forgetting. Once you have forgiven somebody for something, forget it. If it's someone you know – a friend or family member – don't keep bringing it up and reminding them of their mistakes and reminding yourself that you were wronged or offended. If you say you'll forgive, but you won't forget, then you haven't really forgiven at all.

> *The best thing to give your*
> *enemy is forgiveness;*
> *to an opponent, tolerance;*
> *to a friend, your heart;*
> *to your child, a good example;*
> *to a father, deference;*
> *to your mother, conduct that will*
> *make her proud of you;*
> *to yourself, respect;*
> *to all men, charity.*
> - Arthur James Balfour

48. Be a good sport.

This goes for anything in life where there are winners and losers. Remember why we participate in those activities. Most of the time the reason is to have fun, right? Well . . . have fun! We should try not to get so caught up in the competition that we forget why we're involved with that activity.

If you're not a good sport, it's likely that you go around pouting a lot, and you've probably already discovered that you're not very happy when you pout. Join in the fun, and don't let it bother you to lose games or even occasionally lose face when someone has a little harmless fun at your expense. Happy people aren't so proud and uptight that they can't laugh at themselves.

Terry's husband, Allen, likes to laugh (and enjoys pulling an occasional practical joke.) He also likes to observe the way people do things and will often find humor in their minor and sometimes embarrassing mistakes. But it's okay that he does because he doesn't mind also laughing at himself, as Terry explains:

"One time when we were travelling on business in another state with a friend, we stopped at a restaurant to eat lunch. When we were ready to head out, Allen went to the restroom. Our friend and I were standing across the dining area of the restaurant waiting for him to emerge so we could all leave. When he did step out of the restroom back into the dining room we noticed he was trailing a huge piece of toilet tissue on his foot. We began to giggle which made Allen realize there was something wrong with his appearance. While he was trying to discreetly check his zipper, he ran into a huge stack of chairs which made a loud racket and naturally drew the attention of everyone in the restaurant. He hurried out the door, thankful that we'd probably never eat there again.

"As embarrassed as he was, Allen never minds telling that story because he knows it's funny, and he's learned that his ego can stand someone laughing at him, because he laughs with them."

If you like pranks and practical jokes, make sure you don't let them get out of hand. And remember, if you dish it out, you better be ready to take it.

49. Don't let the turkeys get you down.

Accept that there will always be those around you whom you will never be able to please. For whatever reason, you seem unable to do anything which is acceptable to them. Don't waste too much time trying to please people who are the "turkeys" of life.

We all have had to deal with our fair share of turkeys. When writing this section, it was hard to choose which turkey to tell you about, but after some thought, we decided to give the "Turkey Award" to a woman who is not a very happy person, and who never tries very hard to make those around her happy, either.

In the business which Terry and her husband previously owned, they had one customer, in particular, who was a turkey. It seemed nothing could be done to please her.

"We always tried so hard to do our best for her, but we always managed to fall short," explains Terry. "We worked on projects for her several times a year, and it was actually some of the best work our company produced. We always received rave reviews from other people who saw samples of her publication, but she was never completely satisfied. She managed to find *something* wrong *every* time.

"We decided not to let ourselves be bothered about *her* problems. You see, instead of anticipating good results, she was always expecting something to go wrong, so she wasn't surprised when she wasn't satisfied with the work. We pretty much smiled and nodded and made adjustments when we needed to and went on doing the best we could. She ranted and raved, but the interesting thing is, she continued to do business with us and is still doing business at the company we previously owned!"

Some of us feel the need to be liked by everyone. In itself, that's not a bad goal; we should all try to live our lives in a manner which gives no one any reason to dislike us. BUT, *none of us can please everybody all of the time.*

We gave you an example from the business world, but we've all known people in our personal lives who have made it their vocation to find fault and be disagreeable.

What's detrimental to our happiness is obsessing over the

reasons people don't seem to like us. If you're certain you've treated someone fairly and with all respect and have given them no reason to dislike you, then there will occasionally be those around you whom you'll just have to give up on. They won't ever be your friends, and you mustn't let it bother you. Don't expend any energy disliking them; just let it go.

Not all of us are compatible with each other. Not only is it quite exhausting to constantly seek the approval of others, but you're setting yourself up for failure and unhappiness as well.

> *Keep your face to the sunshine and you cannot see the shadow.*
>
> - Helen Keller

*Turkeys would like to make
your life miserable.
Don't let them do it!*

50. Find someone you like working with and work with them.

So, you've weeded out some people with whom you are not compatible. Now, find someone with whom you are compatible and work with that person.

This is exactly how the "Ronnie and Terry team" was born. We discovered that we enjoyed working with each other no matter what we were doing. Whether we were performing in a play at the community theatre where we met or working at the concession stand or even fixing a valve in a toilet, we had fun! (We *really did* fix a toilet at the theatre, and we had a good time doing it.)

It was after we made this discovery that we decided to write this book and prepare our motivational presentation that we also do. Along the way, we distanced ourselves from groups and situations to which we no longer felt we were making a contribution and from which we were not receiving satisfaction. As a result, our happiness level increased.

Aren't you happiest when you're around people you like? It's okay to say there are some people you enjoy being with, and some other people you don't enjoy as much. Find a way to use that to your advantage. Go into business with those you enjoy spending time with. After all, you're going to be spending more waking time with the people you work with than with anyone else so it's much better if you like your co-workers.

You should also belong to organizations that are filled with those who are compatible with you and share many of the same interests. The time you spend volunteering should be enjoyable, not a chore.

In short, don't set yourself up to be unhappy by putting yourself in positions where you'll be spending a lot of time with people whose company you do not enjoy.

51. Here's a motto to think about: "Don't help me, don't hurt me."

This is a saying that Ronnie's dad came up with. Ronnie explains:

"I used to help my dad in his line of work, which is laying carpet. Sometimes I would be at the wrong place at the wrong time. Instead of my dad saying, 'Get out of my way,' he would say, 'If you're not going to help me at least don't hurt me by being in my way while I work.' This was shortened to 'Don't help me, don't hurt me.'

"This is a good way to look at many situations. If you're not helping someone, don't hurt them by sabotaging their efforts. In my situation, I wasn't intentionally trying to be unhelpful, and sometimes, you aren't either, but you're still making things difficult for other people. Sabotage – whether intentional or not – is a negative behavior, and as we all know negative behaviors make it harder to be happy.

"On the same note, don't hang around people you think may be trying to sabotage your efforts because whether they are or not, if you believe it, happiness will not be on your mind."

We believe we should always actively be looking for ways to help everyone in every situation, but sometimes that's not possible, and the best we can do is just stay out of their way!

Sometimes, even when we're doing a good thing, we're in the wrong place at the wrong time!

52. Be consistent.

Be consistent when dealing with people. Consistency helps clear up relationships with others. It enables us to deal with people on a day-to-day basis. We all like dealing with someone who we know will behave the same way every time a situation arises.

Being consistent will add to your own happiness by taking away the 'how do I deal with this situation?' factor. If you're consistent, you'll know how you should handle almost every circumstance.

This is especially important for parents, teachers, and other people who work with children. Children need consistency. They need some things on which they know they can always depend. Provide them with a sense of security and permanence. It's difficult for them to be happy when they're worried about what new, unsettling thing is going to happen in their life tomorrow.

Be consistent with your requests, and make sure that what you're asking is reasonable. If you know in advance that you will make exceptions to certain rules, then don't present those rules as though they are absolute commandments. For example, you set your child's bedtime at nine o'clock. It is a certainty that sometimes this will not apply. You may be away from home at nine o'clock. There may be special visitors at your home who don't get to see your child often. Whatever the reason may be, occasionally your child will miss his or her bedtime. Don't sweat it, and don't make a big deal about it.

If you decide that there are some things that must be done a certain way to insure that mayhem will not rule, then make sure you enforce those requirements. Just let someone get away with breaking an "absolute" requirement, and there goes everyone's happiness out the window. A yelling and screaming match will often ensue, *and* it will be much more difficult to enforce that rule the next time it needs to be enforced.

Being consistent helps bring balance into our lives.

53. Trying to save the world is an impossible task.

Finding true happiness does not mean that we can retreat into our own little space and ignore the world around us. We must interact and help where we can. However, we should never try to be responsible for the entire world and everybody in it. It just can't be done, and anyone attempting to do it will be driven crazy.

Also, what will often happen when someone is trying to save the whole world is that he'll end up not really doing much of anything at all. Those around him, whom he really can assist, fall by the wayside. His goals are so huge that he never seems to get started on them. He plans a lot and accomplishes very little.

Realize that one person can indeed make a big difference, but we must start where we are, right in our own neighborhoods, and have a positive influence on our friends, family, and associates. Our good efforts may change the lives of a great many people, but the changes will happen one person at a time.

In today's technological world, this attitude is sometimes hard to maintain. We see so many more problems than our grandparents did in their younger days. Satellites allow us to view what's happening on the other side of the world, sometimes as it's happening. It's difficult to watch the problems of the world on the nightly news because it can be overwhelming, and we often feel powerless to help. There seems to be *so much* to do. How can a person have knowledge of all of this distress and still be happy?

If we're not careful, the problems of the world can overshadow the problems we have in our local communities, but the key is to concentrate on the things we *can* do to make a difference. We're not suggesting that you become an isolationist, but we do suggest you remember the "serenity prayer," and stop feeling obligated to change the whole world – changing your own little corner of it is difficult enough.

God grant me the serenity to accept the things I cannot change, the courage to change the things I can, and the wisdom to know the difference.

54. Be generous with praise and good wishes.

Do you really want to feel good? Then make someone else feel good! Heaping sincere praise on someone for a job well-done makes everyone happy.

In our fast-paced society with so many things going on, it's often easy to let the accomplishments of others slide by without comment. It's true that sometimes it takes a little effort to go out of your way to say, "Good job!" But once you start the trend, you'll find that it becomes easier. And you'll find it's quite enjoyable, too.

Always be ready to send your best wishes or a word of congratulations. Doesn't it make you happy when someone remembers your birthday, and they send you a card or give you a call? (Everybody likes to feel special.) Well, you can make others happy – and yourself in the process – by becoming the best customer at the greeting card store. (Or even better, make your own cards!)

Take a moment to send a greeting on anniversaries and other special occasions. Sending cards at Christmas is quite common, but you might want to try something new. Send valentines or cards at Easter or on St. Patrick's Day. At Thanksgiving, write to someone and tell them how thankful you are that you know them.

Send a thank you note when someone gives you something or helps you or encourages you. Become an encourager yourself by sending notes of sympathy or to wish someone well. Send a note of congratulations when someone graduates or gets a promotion or gets married or has a baby or . . . whatever! Or give someone a call and tell them in person.

Your life will be so much happier when you begin to take the steps that lead toward putting the feelings of others ahead of your own. When you become secondary in importance to those around you, then strangely enough, true happiness comes to you.

To look up and not down
To look forward and not back
To look out and not in, and
To lend a hand.

- Edward Everett Hale

Chapter Four

Practice Common Sense

Happiness is in your attitude and in your ideas, but it is also in a thing called common sense – that part of life gained by experience and not by any special study. This is the practical stuff that you do every day.

*Be happy in the
smallest, most
mundane parts
of your life.*

55. Don't make life more complicated than it is.

It seems as though life is very complicated these days, and sometimes it truly may be; but the majority of the complications in our lives arise from our own imaginations. Most things can usually be kept pretty simple. Simplify and be happy.

Life is as complicated as we make it. There are some basic truths and beliefs each person lives by. Once we figure out what those truths are for us, it's up to us to live our lives based on those truths.

There are some people who live life in a constant state of agitation because every little detail is a major undertaking from start to finish. Decisions which should require practically no thought at all become a matter for forming a committee or having a group discussion. If a person has time to devote several hours to simple decisions, then he or she has time to accomplish a lot of things that are much more worthwhile.

If someone asks you what time it is, don't tell them how to build a clock; just tell them the time!

Nothing is more wasteful than doing with great efficiency that which should not be done.

- Theodore Levitt
former editor
Harvard Business Review

If this is how you look when you take your child to the playground, you may need to simplify your attitude toward life.

56. Think before you speak and sleep on large decisions.

It is sometimes necessary to put some thought into major decisions which can have a large effect on your life or the lives of others. Decisions about changing jobs, getting married, moving to a new location or other similar things should not be jumped into without some consideration.

Hasty judgments are dangerous. If we rush into things, we can often make decisions or get into situations that we wish we hadn't. This will lead to regret about those decisions *and* to our unhappiness. This does not mean to put off decision-making too long because that can also lead to not being happy. What our ultimate goal should be, as in all areas of life, is to find balance. When we have enough information and have had time to process it, then we can make the decision. We shouldn't stall just because we don't want to face making a decision.

We should never feel forced to make hasty decisions about big questions. Considering all the issues by making a list of pros and cons can sometimes help.

And then, get a good night's rest before making your final determination. Things just seem to take on a new light at the break of day.

Sometimes, if we don't give enough thought to what we're saying, we can get ourselves into situations which we aren't actually prepared to handle.

57. Deal with situations before they reach crisis proportions.

Set realistic deadlines, and meet them. A huge project cannot be accomplished in a few hours. Make time to do a little bit every day instead of staying up all night to finish something which you've had weeks to work on.

When we keep putting off until tomorrow what we can and should do today, little snags can grow into huge predicaments. We should learn how to take action on relatively small matters as quickly as we can.

Don't let an issue get discussed by a lot of people because it often becomes a completely different problem when the story is told and re-told.

Stop potential complications before they even get a chance to get started. Barney Fife of *Andy Griffith Show* fame knew this, and that's why he said problems should be "nipped in the bud." Even though Barney might not exactly be the poster child for happiness, he did get this part of being happy right!

Be a bud-nipper.

The time to remember to bring an oar is <u>before</u> you're in the middle of the lake.

58. Finish one task before starting another.

A lot of unhappiness is caused by having too many things going on all at once. The best way to avoid this problem is to finish one thing before going on to another. It is very frustrating to have unfinished tasks lying around haunting you, practically calling out your name all day long, drawing your attention away from other things you're trying to do.

When we run around like the proverbial chicken with the missing head, we find it very difficult to achieve *any* of our goals. Life seems to become quite overwhelming when we begin to feel as though we aren't getting anything done. On the other hand, a finished task is quite satisfying, because we can then begin a new task and give it all of the energy and time it deserves.

It really helps to start your day by prioritizing the things you need to do and then making a list of those things. Follow your list and mark off items as you finish them. You may have a thing or two left which you need to carry over, but that's okay. It gives you a real sense of accomplishment to see those things get finished and stricken from the list.

Santa <u>has</u> to make a list and check it twice –
otherwise, he'd never get all of his work done!

59. Take a little extra time to do it right the first time.

When we think there's never enough time to do a task right the first time, we discover that finding time to do it over makes us *very* unhappy! Terry remembers a girl in her junior high home economics class who fell victim to this kind of unhappiness.

"When we started our sewing project, there was one friend of mine who was especially dreading it. She had never sewn a stitch in her life and had no desire to do so. (She didn't like to cook, either, so I'm not really sure why she was even in that class which only covered those two subjects, but that's a different story.)

"She chose to make a simple pull-over shirt which was the least complicated pattern she could find. She had actually completed the garment rather painstakingly, but when it came to the very last thing she had to do – tie off the loose threads and clip the ends – she got in a bit of a hurry and clipped a perfect "v" in a fold right in the front of her shirt! It was the only time, before or in the years since, that I've ever heard a bad word escape her lips, but she was *very* unhappy that day."

Probably all of us have firsthand experience with rushing through a job, making a mess of it, and then having to start all over again. When will we ever learn to stop doing the things that make us unhappy? Just like almost everything else that's worthwhile in life, it takes lots of time and practice to break bad habits and develop good ones.

If someone (like your boss) assigns a task, make sure you know exactly what you're being asked to do. Don't belabor the point, but if there's even the slightest chance you may be doing an assigned task the wrong way, find out for sure what the right way is before you do it.

Let's slow down. We shouldn't use an unreasonably long amount of time to finish something, but neither should we feel compelled to speed through projects. Work at organizing your time so that you aren't putting yourself in the position of not having enough time to accomplish what you need to do.

Try not to spend your life always catching your breath because you've been dashing around doing your daily work.

60. Learn how to delegate.

You don't have to do *everything*. There are other people in the world, and quite often, it's very appropriate to solicit their help. This is tough for some of us, because we are accustomed to doing everything by ourselves. (Our rationale is that we want to make sure things are done right.)

We should get over the idea that we are the only ones capable of really doing anything. There are many people who are quite competent, and there comes a time when we must trust others. It's imperative that we learn to delegate tasks so we don't kill ourselves trying to get things done.

For the most part, people want to help; they want to feel like they're part of a team. Make them part of *your* team.

The basis for this bit of advice as part of the road to happiness goes back to the notion that it's difficult to be happy when you're overworked and worn out. It's true that many of us do enjoy our jobs, (both paying and non-paying work) but it's not healthy to exclude other aspects of our lives just so we can work all of the time!

To successfully delegate, try to match up talents and abilities with specific tasks. If you can do this – for yourself and others – everyone will be happier.

We all have certain talents and abilities, and most of us like to use them. In fact, when we work *with* our strengths there is a much better chance we'll be successful at whatever we're doing. Success gives people confidence and a sense of worth and belonging.

So, ask for help if you need it, and allow others to help you when they offer. We shouldn't be so independent that we cheat people out of the opportunity to feel good about themselves by assisting us!

Terry knows firsthand about how difficult it is to accept help.

"I've always been very independent. My mother tells me that even when I was a baby, quite often, I preferred just to be left alone. If I was fussy, and she couldn't figure out what else to do, she would put me in my crib and usually that made me stop crying. I've carried that sort of 'I'll do it my way, thank you' attitude into my adult life.

"In an effort to be better in this regard (and to see if this advice is really worth giving!), I tried asking for someone's help the other day as a little test.

"When my husband and I were first married, I sewed quite a bit. I made most of my own clothes and even tackled making a coat one time. But then we had our daughter and with a heavier workload at home and at my job, I stopped sewing.

"Over the past few years, since I've become involved in community theatre, I have taken to occasionally sewing again to make costumes. Recently, I needed to make a black velvet dress for a play I was going to be in. I found the pattern I wanted, picked out the material and was trying to figure out what to do about lining it. I had already wasted several minutes trying to decide what kind of lining material to get, when I spotted a woman who I didn't really know but had seen several times working as a checker at a local store.

"As she confidently went here and there gathering up what she needed for her sewing project, I thought, 'Now, there's a woman who knows what she's doing. I think I'll just ask her opinion on this lining problem.'

"When I approached her, she was happy to share her knowledge. She had very good suggestions about the lining and a couple of other things I hadn't even thought about, including that I should be sure to use a sharp needle in my machine. That reminded me that I'd been needing to get new needles but had completely forgotten. So I bought new ones before I went home.

"The whole encounter was very positive, and I was glad I had asked for help. I decided that letting others occasionally give me assistance really can make me happy, and that this *really is* good advice we're giving our readers!"

We aren't weak just because we accept someone's help; we are, in fact, quite wise.

61. Never stop learning.

Acquire knowledge like a sponge. If you lose your desire to learn new things, you'll be missing out on happiness you can't even imagine!

You should learn something every day. In fact, you probably already do learn something new every day, but you've just never thought about it. Life is a learning experience. Each day should be a learning experience.

We all know that as we grow older, learning helps keep our minds active and alert, and certainly you've heard the old adage, 'If you don't use it, you'll lose it.' Well, we suggest you use that brain of yours every day – give it a good work out! (We like to say that a brain that is learning is a happy brain.)

While becoming so educated that we approach everything from a strictly intellectual point of view is not much fun, it is also not true that "ignorance is bliss" as you may have heard. Again, balance is the key, but discovering new things and looking at the world with eyes of wonder is very rewarding.

Here are some things you may not know:

Swans have been known to live 300 years.

When the Hebrews (about 2 million people in all) were led by Moses out of Egypt into the Promised Land, the journey took 40 years. If they had walked directly to where they were going, it would have taken them approximately eleven days to be within sight of their final destination.

The Pacific end of the Panama Canal is farther east than the Atlantic end.

62. Be as physically active as you can.

Be sure to exercise not only your mind, but your body as well. While obsession about our bodies is not healthy, a regular schedule of physical activity is good for both the body and the mind.

Develop healthy habits and take care of yourself. How well you feel on a day to day basis (barring serious disease or physical defect) depends mostly on your attitude, but also on how well you take care of your body.

When you exercise it's good for the body and mind, so you can even think of it as pampering yourself. It's good for the body because it releases endorphins which help you feel better. It also helps relieve tension. Exercise gives you more energy to do the things you enjoy doing. It's good for you mentally and emotionally because it clears the mind, and many people use exercise time as meditation or prayer time. All of these things will make you a healthier person which in turn will make you a happier person.

Excesses in eating, smoking, drinking or whatever your particular vice might be will lead to poor health; being in poor health doesn't necessarily mean we'll have an unhappy life, but it does make a happy life harder to achieve.

When a person wakes up in the morning feeling lousy, he finds it difficult to even drag his sorry carcass out of bed much less think there's a prospect of actually *enjoying* the day. But if one wakes up feeling fit and healthy, the day stretches ahead full of possibility and promise.

Even people with the busiest schedules need to find a few minutes to get some exercise every day.

63. Talk to, listen to, read books written by inspirational, happy people.

None of us can really depend on others for our happiness, but happy people are just naturally inspiring so it doesn't hurt our own attitude to spend some time with them.

If you read books about how to become rich, most of them will tell you to hang around rich people to see how they live their lives and then imitate them to become rich. You should do the same if you want to be happy. There are happy people out there, and you can learn from those people. If you're reading happy, inspirational books, it will help you have those kinds of thoughts.

What you concentrate on, what you take into your mind, is basically what comes out of you. If you read depressing books, listen to music which has lyrics that talk about dying, and hang around people who constantly say what terrible shape the world is in — well, face it — you probably aren't going to be a big fireball of happiness. In fact, you'll probably be downright dejected most of the time.

Surround yourself with the good and optimistic things of life, and spend time with people who are happy. Fill your cup with joy, and drink it up!

Surround yourself with happy people.

64. Pay your bills on time and watch your debt.

Most of us go in debt if we want a car or home. Borrowing money can be okay, as long as we don't get carried away. If we get so deep in debt that we start feeling overwhelmed, we find it harder to be happy.

It's bad enough to have a big debt, but there's nothing worse than having a big debt hanging over your head and then having to go to a job every day which you don't enjoy to pay that debt.

Being in debt keeps us in bondage. Being without huge financial obligations gives us so much more freedom, and freedom in all areas of our lives is a major way to attain happiness.

Dodging calls from bill collectors is not a good way to achieve happiness. Take responsibility for your life. Don't spend more than you make, and pay as you go. Those little bills add up so quickly and before you know it, you're in way over your head, and your family life starts to suffer because everyone is fighting over whose fault it is that there's never enough money and – oh, my goodness! Stop running up bills right now before it's too late!

Debt is distressing.

65. Be on time and be dependable.

While you're resolving to be on time paying your bills, decide to be on time wherever you go. In fact, resolve to be an all-around dependable person.

Rushing around is not the way to find happiness. (If you've ever been late to a movie and missed the first five minutes, you know how unhappy you were that you were late.) Schedule things so you can be on time. And don't over-schedule; no one can be in more than one place at the same time. Try not to underestimate how long it will take you to do something or get somewhere. You're not Superman or Wonder Woman, so set realistic goals. This goes for any deadline: a project at work, a dinner date, or your child's school play.

Don't gain a reputation for being undependable. If you tell someone you're going to do something, do it. If you say you're going to be somewhere at a certain time, be there. If your plans change because of circumstances beyond your control, let the other people involved know what's going on.

If you'll do this, you will find that others who are always waiting on you or expecting you to do something will be happier; and anytime you can make others around you happier, it will add to your happiness.

Additionally, if your friends and family can't count on you, they'll eventually give up on you, and they won't include you in their reindeer games. Now, *that* won't make you very happy, will it?

If people are expecting you, do whatever it takes to get there!

66. Be organized.

It's not much fun when you're already late for work and you're running around looking for your other shoe and you can't find your car keys. People start to shout and get angry, and everybody's day is off to a bad start. If this describes your house, it's time to get organized! This is not easy for some people, but it's a skill worth working on. If we organize our lives, we'll find it's much easier to be happy.

Many people spend their whole life going from one crisis to another due to their lack of organization. If your life is always in a crisis because you're not organized, you'll find it harder to be happy because you'll always be thinking of other things besides happiness. (Plus, it's time-consuming always looking for some lost item.)

Being organized doesn't mean we must have everything in our freezers in alphabetical order, but it does mean that we need to have things in our main work areas at least in organized piles so we can find them when we need to. If you don't know how to become organized, find someone who is and ask them for help. (Usually, organized people *love* organizing others. If you've ever seen the *Odd Couple*, you know how happy it would have made Felix to have had the opportunity to organize Oscar!) There are also professional organizers who can whip even the messiest people into shape for a fee.

At home and in the workplace and in groups of all kinds, organization is such a welcome element. Day to day living is simplified and streamlined by an orderly approach. We shouldn't turn our surroundings into a sterile environment with no room for spontaneity and humor, but it's not good to let chaos rule either. By bringing a little order into our lives we can head off a lot of potential problems.

Now, all of you compulsive types, don't use this as an excuse to force your exceptionally high standards of neatness off on unwilling victims. (It's a well-known fact that neat freaks drive non-neat freaks crazy and vice-versa.) Find a balance, and your home will run much more smoothly.

67. Pick up after yourself.

One way to help immensely in your efforts to be organized is to pick up after yourself. We like the saying, "Pick up after yourself – your mother doesn't work here." Well, not even moms should have to be constantly picking up possessions which belong to someone other than themselves!

A mom we know told us a story of a time when her daughter was about four years old and had decided she wasn't going to keep her things picked up in her room. The "discussions" about the situation flew back and forth until one day the mom decided to enlist the dad's help.

Dad had been cutting and burning brush on their farm, and when he came in the house for a break, Mom said, "You've got to help me do something about Mary's room!" Dad went to his daughter's room where yet another discussion ensued, and the end result was that he marched out of the house with an armload of her favorite toys which he told her he intended to burn, but which he actually put in the garage.

As he headed back into the house to check on what he hoped would be the repentant attitude of his daughter, she met him at the door, and she also had an armload of her favorite things. She said, "You might as well burn these, too, because I'm not picking *them* up either!" (Fortunately, no toys were actually harmed, and Mary grew out of this phase.)

When we stop leaving our things lying around just wherever they happen to land and start making an effort to put them where they belong immediately, we discover that we're far less likely to misplace them. We're less frustrated and much happier and have the added bonus of wasting less time searching for our possessions. Each of us should take responsibility for ourselves and what we own.

In a similar vein to picking up your own stuff, make doubly sure you put back what you borrow from others. Always leave things the way you found them and, if possible, in better condition.

The world and all of its inhabitants would be a much nicer place if we would all follow this common sense suggestion.

68. If you loan it, realize it may come back in an altered state from its original condition.

"Never a borrower or a lender be." That's pretty safe advice, but probably not very practical (when you want to borrow something) or very neighborly (when your friends want to borrow from you). So, if people want to borrow your things, and you do loan something, be prepared for *anything*!

"My daughter learned this lesson a couple of years ago," explains Terry. "She had an acquaintance who spent the night with us right after school was dismissed for summer vacation. I took her and Tracy to town the next day, and this girl wanted to borrow a pair of Tracy's shoes and some of her clothes. And not just *any* clothes would do. She rejected the first shirt Tracy offered because it wasn't a name brand, and she also wanted to wear a pair of Tracy's more expensive leather shoes.

"When Tracy said good-bye to this girl at the end of the day, she also said so-long to the items she had loaned her. Attempts to reach the girl were futile because she didn't have a phone. When school started again in the fall, I kept telling Tracy to please have the girl bring at least the shoes to school. Tracy repeatedly tried to get through to her, but she kept 'forgetting' to bring the shoes.

"Finally, several months later, she had Tracy stop by her locker where she showed her two pair of worn-out shoes, neither of which were Tracy's! None of the borrowed items were ever returned."

Lots of folks are just not as careful with things as you are, and even though they don't intend to, sometimes they just wreck whatever they get their hands on. And even when people are being careful, accidents do happen.

So, keep in mind, lending can be a frustrating thing. It's usually best for your own happiness to keep your expectations low when it comes to how others will treat your things. If you have something which is *really* important to you, perhaps you shouldn't loan it out. If you know someone who has a poor record when it comes to destroying things or returning borrowed items, then don't loan to them unless you're really a glutton for punishment!

69. Get it in writing.

Even between friends, maybe *especially* between friends, if issues of loaning money or valuable property exchanges are involved, don't depend on verbal agreements. The contracts can be quite simple, but you still need to have certain things in writing. That way, everyone involved will know what is expected, and misunderstandings will be headed off.

Keep accurate records of everything, and don't sign anything without thoroughly reading it first.

Partnerships should always be as equal as possible. It's best not to go into a business venture with anyone (good friends included) if you have more at stake than the other party. You not only stand to lose more should something go awry, the other person has less emotional attachment and therefore might not be as motivated to succeed.

Terry speaks from experience:

"My husband and I have been involved in partnerships in two businesses since we've been married; one was successful and one was not.

"The first business we had was with a good friend of ours who was single at the time and didn't own anything which could be used to secure a loan. My husband and I owned property which was what we used as the only collateral to borrow the money to start the business.

"All of the proper paperwork was drawn up to make both us and him responsible for repaying the loan, but the fact remained that it was *our* property at stake, and when the business failed to support two families, my husband and I were the ones left to pay off all of the bills. It was an expensive lesson for a young married couple to learn, but when we went into business again with new partners, you can bet we didn't make the same mistake again! The second time around turned out to be a successful and profitable venture for us and our partners because it was an equal relationship."

It's pretty simple, basic stuff, but this is all advice which can help ward off headaches, heartaches and hard feelings.

70. Dress comfortably.

This may seem like a strange thing to include as one way to be happy, but it's true that it's quite difficult to be happy when you're uncomfortable.

Make sure your attire is appropriate for the occasion, but don't feel forced to follow fashion fads and rules which are quite often ridiculous and unnecessary (and *not* conducive to your happiness).

For example, women, in particular, often shove their feet into shoes which must surely have been invented by torture experts and walk a few miles around the office every day with cramped toes and their feet at unnatural angles. Sore feet and legs, stress, backaches and poor toe health are the result. For crying out loud, even if your job requires that you "dress up," get some comfortable shoes!

There are plenty of ways to dress acceptably in any situation which do not cause discomfort.

You might even try being brave and starting a few *comfortable* fashion trends of your own.

Ah . . . comfort.

71. Take a vacation.

This is an easy, but sometimes forgotten, method of being happy. We get so caught up in living our lives or working at our jobs that we forget to have fun. Sometimes, we think that our workplace will fall apart without us. Actually, a vacation can help clear your mind and make you *more productive* at home and at work.

There is nothing so relaxing and refreshing as getting away from everything for awhile. Don't put yourself in debt to do it, but find a way to get away from your everyday routine. Whether you travel near or far, make it fun.

Don't take a lot of unrealistic expectations along with you or you'll likely be disappointed. And don't try to do everything. For example, it's not generally a good use of vacation time to go three hours out of your way to see the world's biggest rubber band. If it's cheap, and right on your way, though, we say go for it!

Terry describes such a vacation incident:

"One of the fondest vacation memories that I have (well *fond* may be a strong word) is when our family pulled off the highway we were on to see 'the world's largest buffalo.' Wow! What a buffalo – it *was huge*! And there was a white one, too. We laughed a lot and had a good time."

Try not to be compulsive on vacation. Let things just happen and have fun. *Rest* while you're gone. That way, you won't end up back home recovering from your time off.

Take a break from your usual surroundings.

Here are a few words about common sense, from someone who could easily be called the master of common sense, Abraham Lincoln:

Do not worry. Eat three square meals a day, say your prayers, be courteous to your creditors, keep your digestion good, steer clear of biliousness, exercise, go slow, and go easy. Maybe there are other things that your special case requires to make you happy, but, my friend, these I reckon will give you a good life.

Chapter Five

Love Your Friends & Family

You know them (do you really?), you love them (well, sometimes, anyway). They're your friends and family.

They can be
the source of
your greatest
happiness . . .

(or worst headaches . . .
the choice is yours)

72. Marry a friend.

If you're already married, we hope you married a friend. If not, take some time to become your spouse's best friend – you'll both be so much happier!

We are very dear friends to each other, but Terry's *best* friend is her husband, Allen, and Ronnie's *best* friend is his wife, Tammie. We wouldn't have it any other way!

If you're not yet married, but you would like to be, look for a life partner by looking for someone you like to be with; search out a friend. Find someone with whom you have common interests. Don't rule out developing a romantic relationship with any of your friends just because they are your friends. There may be a perfect life partner for you among the ranks of your current friends.

A successful, long-term relationship depends on many things. Some good ingredients to bring into a marriage are: cooperation, mutual respect, love, laughter, loyalty and the enjoyment of being in the company of your spouse. Aren't those some of the same things you seek in a friend?

Romance in marriage is certainly conducive to happiness, but there's plenty of time for candlelit dinners *after* you're married. You can always work your way up to that; you don't have to burn up *all* the candles before you wed.

Be a buddy to your spouse.

73. Love your children.

This is the number one commandment for raising children. Should you decide to have children of your own, please appreciate and adore them. It is such a *privilege and a blessing* to have a child; we can never forget that. They are the most precious of any resource.

Children do not choose to be born, they cannot pick what family they will be a part of, nor do they decide what their own very unique personality will be. They must be accepted for who they are and never blamed because they are not someone else.

People often wonder how to raise their children. They want to know how to deal with unruly behavior and other unpleasant situations. The one word answer is "love." A child who is raised in a loving home will be okay. This is *not* a child who has been *bought* everything to show that he is loved or a child who is merely *told* all the time that he is loved, but it is a child who is truly loved.

If every decision you make for or about your child is done out of love, the child will be happy. (He or she may be *temporarily* miffed, but in the long-term they will be happy.) Too many children have been raised in homes where decisions are based on time conservation and not love. It's so easy for parents to turn on the television and let whatever's coming over the airwaves (or in through cable) entertain, educate and guide their children. Is this a decision made out of love? No. It's made out of convenience for the parent. Later, we *all* pay the price for that convenience.

Children deserve to have freedom, but for their own happiness and development, they also deserve to be disciplined and instilled with a set of high moral standards. Ground them in tradition. Children who grow up without love mixed with appropriate discipline often turn into unhappy adults with no self-control and end up making a lot of other people, including their parents, quite unhappy also.

It is *not* loving your children to grant them their every wish, while catering to their every whim. They become so demanding and obnoxious that no one wants to be around them. They're miserable, and they don't know why.

What are some things to give children that won't spoil them? Hugs. Kisses. A secure environment. Praise for a job well done. Lots of love. Lavish *love* on your children, but not every material possession they happen to desire at the moment. Teach your child to be a contributing member of your household, and he'll learn what it is to be a responsible citizen.

If you want to be happy and raise happy children, you need to make sure you love your children. Many mistakes made in child raising can be compensated for if the child feels loved.

A friend of ours told us a story of a Christmas when she was just a little girl. Her folks had arranged with her Uncle "Leroy" to dress up in a Santa Claus costume, show up at their house and do the usual "What would you like for Christmas?" routine.

After his mission was successfully accomplished, Uncle Leroy headed out the front door. After a moment's hesitation, our friend was able to formulate a plan that entailed following Santa out the door to catch a glimpse of his sleigh and eight tiny reindeer. She bolted toward the porch before anyone could stop her.

Uncle Leroy was just rounding the corner of the house when he saw her running toward him. He took off like a flash, forgetting that a big woodpile stood between him and the safe cover of darkness.

Our friend arrived at just about the time he was picking himself up and limping away. When she returned to the house, she commented, "When Santa cusses, he sounds a lot like Uncle Leroy!"

You might say it was a bit unfortunate or even a drastic mistake that she saw everyone's childhood hero in very unheroic form that night, but because there was enough love and good intentions in the situation, everything was fine, and there was no long-term damage.

Even if you do not have children yourself, like Uncle Leroy you can be a positive influence on the children around you: nieces, nephews, students, neighborhood kids. They need all the help they can get as they navigate the rough seas of life.

74. Marital problems aren't solved by having children.

Under perfect circumstances, children would only be conceived because a loving family desires to be a part of the miracle of bringing into the world another child whom they intend to love and nurture. Unfortunately, we don't live in a perfect world, and children are born into all kinds of circumstances, some good and some bad.

One of the very worst reasons for having a child is the notion that having a baby will strengthen a shaky relationship. If a couple has a faltering marriage, they should deal with the issues which are causing the problems, and not attempt to hide the issues by having a child. They will not be happier; they will probably only become more miserable. They'll still have the old problems, they'll have a child who depends on them, they'll have new problems, and they'll quite likely have a divorce. Then the child will also have to deal with all the problems that come with being a child from divorce.

Even the very best marriages sometimes encounter difficulties when a new baby arrives, so don't be so naive as to think a weak marriage will improve if a couple has a child. Couples should have children because they *want* children.

Also, please don't be naive enough to think that having a child will make whoever helped you conceive that child love you if he or she doesn't love you already. There are too many broken hearts and lives which are testimony to the fact that looking for love by having a child doesn't work. There are millions of sad children in the world whose parents made that mistake.

Children are the source of some of the happiest times in our lives, but no one should have a child just to pursue happiness.

75. Don't have sex looking for love.

Just as having a child with someone will not necessarily make that person love you, having sex with someone is even less of a guarantee that he or she will love you. So many young people, in particular, make this mistake, and often they regret it the rest of their lives. For any circumstance outside of a healthy marriage, sex merely complicates a relationship.

Generally, if a person finds love, he or she is one step closer to finding happiness. But sex and love must not be confused. A person can be physically attracted to someone, and it may not be love. If you're thinking about having sex looking for love, hoping that the love will make you happy, don't do it. The love may never be there. Sex complicates the issue of love, and it can also complicate life with worry about the consequences.

You don't have to have sex to date someone. You don't even have to kiss on the first date. The courtship can be such a happy time. You should concentrate on the person you're dating. Hold hands with them; feel their hand in yours. Walk with your arms around each other. Think how empty your hands and arms feel when you're not holding them. Get to know them as a person, not as a sex object. Find out what they like, what they don't like.

There might be sexual chemistry on those dates, but that's what makes courtship so much fun. Just because there's sexual attraction, it doesn't mean you have to act on it. You can always decide to have sex, but once you have it, you can never go back. Waiting for the right person and then waiting to have sex will help uncomplicate your life and help you be happier and healthier.

Abstinence before marriage is a good thing, not an old-fashioned notion, and it's not expecting too much of teenagers to ask them to develop sexual self-control. While the excitement of a sexual experience may seem to be worth the consequences, the stakes are just too high. Aside from the regret and guilt which many people suffer, there are other risks, including pregnancy and sexually-transmitted diseases which we all know have become quite deadly.

Why put your life in danger for a brief feeling of excitement that a sexual encounter brings? Some risks are *not* worth taking.

76. Give to your family instead of your job.

This is a concept that is often overlooked on a daily basis in today's world as careers have taken the top priority in some people's lives. This has happened for two reasons. One is the money factor: people want and need to provide for their families. The other reason is that people want to do well in their chosen career. Neither is a bad goal. It's when we put those goals ahead of our family's happiness that the problems arise.

Providing for the physical needs of our families is good, but we must not forget to also give them our time and love. If you have a family and also want to get ahead in your chosen career, you need to remember that you made the decision to get married and have children. They should come first in your life. People trying to find happiness need to look at this closely. You may find that happiness is already in your family home, but you have forgotten because you've become too busy with your job.

You should not steal from your family to give to anything. (This includes your hobbies. Finding a hobby you enjoy is quite satisfying, but constantly pursuing a hobby which excludes your family is not healthy.) Your spouse and your children should always be more important to you than what you do for a living or do for fun. You shouldn't make the excuse that you work like a dog 80 hours a week, "for them – so they'll have more."

We can tell you this, they don't want more *things*, they want *you*! They want you home for the evening meal. They want your undivided attention while they tell you the ups and downs of their day. They want you at the ballet recitals and the school plays and the little league games and all the other stuff that kids do.

If you constantly find yourself saying, "I can't right now, I'm busy," then you're probably way too busy! Back off your career and your outside activities, and give your family the attention they deserve. They'll be happier. You'll be happier. When your children are grown, you won't live with the regret of wishing you had spent more time with them when they were young.

77. If you love someone "hold on loosely" and make sure you give them room to grow.

We must trust those we love; it's one of the most basic ingredients of true devotion. Lack of trust in a relationship is very sad and usually leads to a whole host of other problems.

So often, people are held back by jealous mates who won't allow them the freedom to try new things and expand their life experiences. Even when there is no physical restraint, there is emotional pressure that is just as disabling. We shouldn't put those we love in the uncomfortable position of feeling they must choose between loyalty to us and doing something they really want to try. That kind of choice only leads to resentment.

Remember the saying from the 1970s that went something like this: "If you love something, allow it to go free. If it doesn't come back, it was not meant to be, but if it does, then cherish it." And what a wonderful idea that is!

Love is not possessing, and possessing is not happiness. Trust *can* put us at risk of being hurt, but it's a chance we must take. If someone betrays your trust, then deal with the betrayal. Talk to the person about the betrayal, and forgive him. Take a hard look at your relationship and at the betrayal, and decide if you can stay in the relationship. If you decide to stay in the relationship, you must trust that person again for the relationship to work. If you don't forgive *and forget* in this situation, you will find yourself re-arguing the issue over and over.

We must allow those around us to have freedom to grow. When we jealously try to hang onto someone with everything we have, controlling his or her every move, then we'll smother whoever we're hanging onto and lose them forever. Trying so hard to hold on that tight, makes a person very tired and unhappy. This includes friends, family, spouses, anyone with whom we desire to have a close relationship.

Terry remembers one time when she was a child, helping her mother unpack her older sister's horse collection from a storage box. There were all different kinds, including porcelain horses which were quite fragile.

"My mom told me to be very careful and hold on tight so I wouldn't drop one and break it. Well, I didn't drop any of them, but I held onto one so tightly that I broke its leg off! It was a crushing way to discover that hanging onto something too tightly can be just as destructive as letting go."

If someone you love has not betrayed your trust, don't *assume* that he or she will let you down. Jealousy and suspicion are not parts of healthy relationships, and they are not behaviors which make you happy. Let those around you have the freedom to grow and change and be who they are meant to be. Don't force anyone into your own mold, your own idea of what they should be doing with their lives. Let those you love have other interests, other friendships, and your own relationship with them will be strengthened by the variety in your lives.

If you can't do these things, you need to take a look at your love for the person in question. True love *does* have trust, and if you don't have trust you will always be unhappy.

I do what you want to do,
Say what you want to say,
Be who you want me to be,
Honey that ain't love to me.

lyrics from the Reo Speedwagon song
"That Ain't Love"
written by Kevin Cronin
from *The Hits* album
Fate Music (ASCAP) ©1986

78. Never betray someone's trust.

It is an awesome responsibility to be completely trusted by someone. It means they have decided that they love you to a much greater degree than most people are ever loved. If you have someone who loves you to that extent, never betray their trust. Because, unless you are truly heartless, your life will be completely miserable knowing you have hurt them by your actions.

Re-establishing trust after a major violation of it is a long and arduous process, one we would certainly not wish on anyone who is seeking to be happy. Developing the habit of considering the consequences of your actions before you do something is helpful in many areas of your life, especially in the area of remaining loyal to your loved ones.

There are many ways to violate a bond of trust, and you probably already know what they are for you. Go into situations with your eyes open, and don't be naive about the intentions of others. Often, people end up doing things they wish they hadn't not because of one big mistake all at once, but because of one minor indiscretion after another. "Innocent" comments or glances turned into more than they bargained for.

Like an expensive vase, trust is hard to obtain, very fragile, and even if it's repaired, it's never the same once it's broken.

79. A person who is in control of his life has a better chance of being happy.

Relationships require a balance of give and take – we should not have to give more than we take, but neither should we take more than we give. That can mean we're quite selfish, which is not good, or it can also mean we're far too dependent – also not good.

Total dependency is devastating to happiness. Those who rely too much on others can become so disabled that they cannot function by themselves, which is certainly a frightening prospect.

You should be as independent as you can, and have confidence in yourself. This does not mean you should never ask for help, but it does mean you should not ask others for help regarding every decision or problem you encounter. If you're confident in making your own decisions, it will be easier for you to make the decision to be happy.

"Empowering" ourselves has become quite a catch phrase in the last few years, but don't dig too deeply into the psychological aspects of what it means. Allow yourself to take responsibility for *you* and *your actions*. Know that your opinion counts as much as anyone else around you, and that you are quite valuable as a person.

Never allow others to dominate your life.

Rabbits of the world unite!

80. No one ever deserves to be hit.

Most of this book is aimed at those people who are basically well-adjusted, but just need a little gentle reminder of what it takes to be happy. But we decided to include these pages because there are many families leading a double life. For all practical appearances, they are happy and doing okay, but the secrets they hide behind the closed doors of their homes are devastating; they are victims of physical abuse.

If you are in a relationship where you are the hitter, STOP!! You must break the chain of abuse. Make the decision that will change your life forever. As long as you are controlling others through abuse, you will not be happy. You may need professional help to stop. Get help if that's what it takes, but *whatever it takes*, do it. Only when you stop the abusive behavior can you start down the road to happiness.

If you are the person who is being hit, get out of the relationship, NOW!! Whoever is hitting you has probably promised to stop in the past, but that person continues to hit you. You cannot be happy as long as you are being abused. *You do not deserve to be hit.* It doesn't matter what you've done or what you've said, you should not be hit for your actions.

If you are being abused by someone you love who claims to love you, we plead with you to leave that relationship and seek immediate help. Sometimes families *are* able to reunite *after* professional counseling for everyone in the family, but you can't hang on, holding onto that hope because your time may be running out. Leave first, then seek counseling. This is an issue beyond happiness; it could most certainly be a matter of life and death.

We're reminded of a story we heard recently of a woman who suffered physical abuse from her husband for many years. Her family knew the situation and begged her to leave every time they saw her wearing sunglasses to hide her bruised face and blackened eyes. She could only reply that she couldn't leave him because she loved him.

As it turns out, she loved him right up until the day he beat her so badly that she lay on the sofa in their living room, unable to call for help and died. He never made an attempt to help her or call for assistance.

It may not be an easy decision to leave, but you can never even approach the notion of happiness until you do it. If you need assistance or need more information, many communities have shelters and/or hotlines for battered and abused women and children.

The Domestic Abuse Hotline number is 1-800-799-7233.

81. Guilt is a poor vacation destination.

In other words, don't go on guilt trips!

Another way to look at it is this: family is important in all of our lives, but we don't have to feel obligated to family just because they are our family.

Our family helps us identify where we come from and, ideally, gives us a strong foundation for life. Families can give us some of our best memories and help us find happiness.

Now that we've said something positive, let's get down to business about families.

Families can also give us some of our worst moments in life. One thing they can do to make us unhappy is send us on a "guilt trip." We've probably all experienced guilt trips, which are basically one way that others use to try to control our lives. Family guilt trips are the most unpleasant because typically your family knows you best. Whether they're trying to get you to do something or go somewhere or do their dirty work or change your behavior, they've had many years to get to know you and how to press your guilt buttons.

To compound the problem, occasionally what they say may even have a grain of truth to it. But your response cannot be that you beat yourself over the head with the information. If there is a valid point to what they say, then perhaps you might want to think about making a change in your life. But as a general rule, they're just seeking out things to jab at you with. Don't buy into their problems.

Genuine love and concern for your family is definitely a good thing. Feeling obligated to treat certain "difficult" relatives a particular way simply because you had the misfortune of being born into the same family is not especially healthy. Be as cordial as you can, but don't allow yourself to be manipulated by anyone with ulterior motives whether they're related to you or not.

If you want to be a happy, you've got to see the guilt trip for the creature it is. When you see a guilt trip coming, label it a guilt trip and then deal with it as such. If you don't want to do the thing your family is trying to get you to do, don't do it. Once you take control of your life and stop letting people use guilt to get to you, you will be a happier person.

The family members trying to control you may not be happy with your new found independence, but this is one case where making others happy will not add to your happiness! Controlling people are unhappy by their own choice, and there may not be much you can do to help them anyway. (You might try giving them a copy of this book!) Tell them why you're not going on any more guilt trips. Tell them you've unpacked your guilt trip baggage, and you're in control of your life and your happiness. They're just going to have to find their own happiness without attempting to send you on a guilt trip.

Live your life with a clean conscience and be guilt-free.

The comedy team of Mike Nichols and Elaine May had a routine which dealt with guilt trips. Even though seeing them do this phone-conversation routine is funnier than just reading it, we think you'll get the message.

Son: Hello?

Mother: Hello, Arthur? This is your mother. Do you remember me?

Son: Mom, I was just going to call you. Is that a funny thing? Do you know I had my hand on the phone. . . .

Mother: Arthur, you were supposed to call me *last* Friday.

Son: Honey, I know. I just didn't have a second, and I could cut my throat.

Mother: Arthur I sat by that phone all day Friday.

Son: I was working . . .

Mother: . . . and all day Friday night . . .

Son: I know, I just . . .

Mother: . . . and all day Saturday

Son: I was in the lab . . .

Mother: . . . and all day Sunday. And your father finally said to me, "Phyllis, eat something. You'll faint." I said, "No Harry. No, I don't want my mouth to be full when my son calls me."

Son: Mom . . .

Mother: And you never called.

Son: Mother, I was sending up a rocket. I didn't have a second.

Mother: Well, it's always something, isn't it?

Son: All right, Honey. Look please . . .

Mother: Look Arthur, I'm sure all the other scientists there have mothers. And I'm sure that they all find time after their breakfast or before their count off . . .

Son: Down.

Mother: . . . to pick up a phone and call their mothers.

Son: Honey, listen, *now* you have me on the phone . . .

Mother: And you know how I worry.

Son: Well, that's the point.

Mother: I read in the paper that you're still losing them.

Son: Mother . . . Mother, *I* don't lose them!

Mother: I nearly went out of my mind.

Son: Honey, listen, I want . . .

Mother: I thought, "What if they're taking it out of his pay?"

82. Get a pet.

Pets cannot replace human friendship, but they can make you very happy because they love unconditionally.

Smaller pets (nearer the bottom of the food chain, if you'll pardon the expression, like birds and lizards and rodents) may not have as much to offer as a dog or a cat, for instance, but they can still provide companionship; and their total dependence on you for their survival can instill in you a real sense of responsibility and being needed. Dogs and cats can be your true friends. We won't get into the 'which is best – dog or cat?' debate because Terry has dogs and Ronnie has a cat, and the merits of both species are many.

Sometimes life can seem unsure, and we may not know who to trust or who to talk to. A pet can be the answer to those problems. When you come home every night, and your pet meets you at the door, it can make a bad day better. Your pet will sit and listen to you, and you don't have to worry who they're going to tell.

Terry's special fondness for Dalmatians is a result of having a beautiful one for a pet when she was a child.

"When I was one year old, someone gave our family a Dalmatian, which we promptly named 'Freckles.' He was also a year old and was my constant companion until he died when we were both 17. Over the years, I had several cats as pets – the most memorable one was a big, yellow tomcat, which I named 'Peachy Sue' – but no other pet, was more important to me than Freckles. He was the best!

"I grew up in a rural area with no close neighbors, and the *youngest* of my three sisters is 19 years older than me. As a result, when I was a child I didn't have close friends or brothers and sisters to play with. But I did have my dog, and he was my best buddy.

"In addition to being a lot of fun, he ate anything I ate, especially seeming to enjoy my leftover apple cores. (He only ate *my* apple cores, not anyone else's.) He loved to run and play, but when I was in trouble or sad, he sensed it and sat quietly by my side, silently consoling me.

"Freckles didn't know a lot of 'parlor tricks,' but he was very smart. As he got older, he lost his hearing, and my dad communicated with him by using a kind of simple, doggie sign language that my dad made up. (My dad promises that it's true!)

"I don't suppose Freckles was really any more special than any of the thousands of other dogs that have been constant companions to lucky kids all over the world, but the memory of his loyalty and sweetness will be in my heart forever."

There really is nothing like the unconditional love of a pet to help make you happier. Nursing homes, hospitals, and other long-term care facilities have discovered that there are many benefits for their patients using "pet therapy."

People with pets tend to live longer, happier lives so you might give it a try.

Pets have lots to offer.

83. Choose happy, life-loving friends.

Good friends make life worth living. Many people you become acquainted with will become "projects" for you. Their life is full of problems, questions, crises and seemingly one major disaster after another. They often need a shoulder to cry on, and if you can be supportive of them during their trials, you're doing a very good thing. Don't wallow with them; lift them out of the mire. Just make sure that you don't take on too many friends who are your projects. Because even though you have the satisfaction of helping them out, they can also be a drain on your energy. One or two is plenty for anyone!

Instead, choose friends who have a positive outlook on life and only once in awhile need counseling from you because of a problem they've encountered, and ones who are willing to support you when you occasionally need a kind word. Being around happy, successful people with whom you have common interests will make you happy, too.

Vibrant friends can make such a difference in life. If a person chooses friends who are happy, he'll find it's much easier to choose happiness. If he has friends who are negative and who complain all of the time, he'll find that he's drawn into that negative behavior which makes it harder to be happy.

The love and support of good friends can make the impossible, possible. If you're fortunate enough to find a good friend in life, make sure you're a good friend in return. This means being trustworthy and loyal among many other things.

Happiness is not only having a friend, but in being a friend.

*It's fun to hang out
with friends who
are happy!*

I do not wish to treat friendships daintily, but with roughest courage. When they are real, they are not glass threads or frostwork, but the solidest thing we know.

- Ralph Waldo Emerson
  from "Friendship: An Essay"
  1841

Chapter Six

Decide What Really Matters

There are a great many things in life which are of small consequence. Seek each day to

> *discover which*
> *things are truly*
> *important and*
> *which are not.*

84. Always try to see the big picture in your daily life.

Taking the big picture view of life is of the utmost importance to personal happiness. In fact, next to just *deciding* to be happy, this is probably the most important thing a person can do to actually achieve happiness. It cannot be over-emphasized that most of what happens to us is of really no consequence in the long-term.

Life can be very complicated sometimes. We encounter so many people with a vast array of problems, and their personalities often clash with our own. All of these things can overwhelm us and make us lose sight of our happiness.

It takes some practice to get over being disturbed by all of the little things that happen in life. If you do start feeling overwhelmed and unhappy, take a step back and ask yourself what is really important. To help in this regard, try to decide if things which are upsetting you will matter a year from now. How about six months from now? Next week? Many things that upset you today won't even matter *tomorrow*!

There are forces at work which are far greater than we are. We must decide which force will rule our lives by choosing to either live in faith or live in fear. By faith, we realize there are larger things in the total picture than just the tiny piece we can see today. Fear causes the smallest issues to become larger than life in our own minds.

Remember, don't sweat the small stuff of life, and when you get right down to it, *most* of it is small.

Looking at the big picture can make life take on a whole different perspective.

85. This too shall pass.

We definitely believe we can be happier every day if we try, but we aren't so naive as to think everyone will be happy all of the time. It's impossible to be happy every second of every day because trials and temptations are part of the package.

We all have to face problems every day we live. Some problems are bigger than others. In fact, some seem as if they have no solution. But if we keep in mind that every problem we face will eventually be over, and we will come out of it stronger, it will be easier to face the problem. The secret to maintaining happiness is not dwelling on the bad things of life, but concentrating on the good.

Some difficult things come into our lives so that we can learn and grow from them. Others happen because of our own actions. But whatever the reason that there is unpleasantness, it doesn't help to dwell on the unpleasantness *or* the reason. Just trust that there are better days ahead and go on with life, always searching for the things which are lasting and eternal, discarding that which is temporary.

We have a friend who is a story-teller and often has words of wisdom for specific situations. One time when an organization we were in was facing an uncertain future, she told a story about a man who lived in a kingdom where the penalty for stealing the king's horse was death. One day, the king's horse escaped from its stable and showed up at the man's house. The man didn't know it was the king's horse and rejoiced at his good fortune in finding such a fine animal.

The king didn't know his horse had merely run away, and he sent his men to find the thief who had taken his horse. They eventually discovered the horse in the man's possession and, despite his protests that he had *found* the horse, it was decided he should be executed for the theft.

The man said to the king, "Wait! I'll make a deal with you. Let me live, and I'll keep the horse for a year and teach it to sing.

If you come to me in a year and the horse isn't singing, you can have the horse, and I'll accept the punishment."

The king was skeptical, but intrigued, so he agreed to the man's proposal. The man's friends said, "Are you *crazy*? What kind of deal is that?"

The man replied, "I *was* facing certain death, and this way, at least I have one more year to live. A lot can happen in a year. I might die of natural causes. The king might die, and I would be released from the sentence. Who knows? *The horse might sing.*"

As hard as it is to believe, some good thing can come out of even the worst situation. If you live with the philosophy that there is always hope and things will get better, you will be happier.

(And it doesn't hurt to visualize a singing horse.)

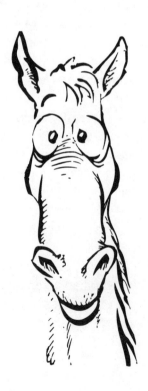

86. Live for the moment.

There is no other point in time which will be exactly like the one you're living right now. There are opportunities and chances you'll never have again. There are joys, and maybe a few sorrows, too, unique to today. Our advice: carpe diem – seize the day, live for the present.

There is a time to dream of the future and a time to remember the past, but the present is all we really have, so make the best of it. Living in the past, constantly re-opening old wounds and re-hashing old arguments, can accomplish nothing. Without time travel, the past cannot be changed; so don't dwell on it! Leave it behind, and go on with life.

Always living for the future is no better. While it is important to have dreams and goals, don't be lulled into a life of no action in the present by only concentrating on the future. Because there is, of course, no promise of tomorrow. After we're gone, we'll never be remembered for all the things we *planned* to do, we'll only be remembered for what we actually accomplished.

By living each day as if it is our last, we'll have a new appreciation of today, and every day we live will become more special. Everything will also take on a new sense of urgency, and we'll be more likely to accomplish those tasks we've been "putting off until tomorrow."

Today is a wonderful day; use it wisely.

One of the illusions of life is that the present hour is not the critical, decisive hour. Write it on your heart that every day is the best day of the year. He only is rich who owns the day, and no one owns the day who allows it to be invaded with worry, fret and anxiety. Finish every day, and be done with it. You have done what you could.

- Ralph Waldo Emerson

87. Don't just dream it, be it.

Dreaming is great, but it's only half the picture. The other half is pursuing your dreams. Take all those things that you keep projecting will happen in the future, and start to make them happen right now!

Mankind has always had dreamers, but the ones we remember are the ones who followed their dreams, the doers. If you dream it, and you really want it, go for it. It may mean some sacrifices, but anything worthwhile is worth the sacrifice.

Do you have plans and dreams that are so big they seem overwhelming? Remember the old proverb, "a journey of a thousand miles begins with a single step," and take that first step. If you have an idea, don't just toss it out for others to do, get in there and lead the way. The only way you're going to live your dream is to be a doer. Working toward a dream is a great way to find happiness.

The Ronnie and Terry partnership began with a single step, and we've walked a long way to get where we are. As we started to realize after working together in community theatre for awhile that we had many of the same goals and aspirations, we began looking for a way to implement them. We decided that two heads are better than one, and that the team approach might give us a unique angle in the speaking market. We started doing a few speaking engagements together in our hometown, and we gradually branched out. We even announced our plans to go into the speaking business together as we were emceeing a local talent show, and everyone in the audience became a part of what we were planning to do. The support and encouragement we got was a great boost to our enthusiasm.

One of the saddest things in life is a dream unfulfilled. Be in the business of making dreams come true – for yourself and for those around you. What a joyous moment it is when you realize your dream has come to pass, and you're living that which previously was just a fantasy.

88. Never look at the grass on the other side of the fence (unless you know there's a gate to get there).

Sometimes, things that we think might be dreams of ours, are really just envy of what someone else has. Some of the things that look attractive to us are only enticing because they belong to someone else, and we can't have them. Pining life away over things that we cannot have is not the same thing as dreaming.

People often make themselves miserable looking at what other people possess, but happiness must start with being content and thankful for what we have *right now*. If you aren't happy when you're poor, you won't be happy when you're rich. Happiness is not dependent on what you have or don't have. Happiness starts with you.

However, wanting a better life is often the start of some really great dreams. It's okay to look at the grass on the other side of the fence; just don't keep staring at it if you're not willing to walk the fence line and find that gate!

89. Accept that you will make mistakes in life.

The only person who doesn't make mistakes is a dead one! We all make mistakes. To get a grip on happiness, we shouldn't allow ourselves to wallow in our errors in judgment and start to feel guilty about how rotten we are. But neither should we continue to make the same mistakes over and over again.

The good thing about a mistake is that we should be able to learn from it how not to make the same mistake again. Some people seem to never learn from their lapses in judgment. They keep making the same mistakes over and over, and then they can't figure out why they're unhappy. Other people make mistakes and then they constantly relive them, not being able to forgive themselves, continually dwelling on the past. They're not happy, either. If we want to be happy, we've got to deal with our mistakes by repenting and forgiving (ourselves and others).

Repenting has evolved over the years into a mostly religious act, almost a tradition, meaning the same thing as saying, "I'm sorry." But repenting means not only feeling regret for having done something wrong, but vowing to change our minds about doing that wrong thing again.

Grow from your mistakes, and become a better person. Go on with living your life. And if you do happen to make the same mistake twice. . . well, promise yourself it will not continue to be a habit, count yourself in the company of a few billion folks who have ever lived on the planet, and start the whole process all over again.

90. Realize your limitations and go on.

We're not all the same. We have different talents and abilities, and we have different weaknesses and limitations as well. We shouldn't make ourselves miserable because we look at those around us and wish we could be like them. It's a great enough challenge to find our true selves and what it is we're supposed to be doing with our own lives without constantly comparing ourselves to everyone else.

Face it, there are some things at which many of us will never excel. You may desire to be a star on the Chicago Bulls, but if you're five feet tall and don't possess some really *exceptional* basketball skills, it's never going to happen. It doesn't mean you're less important than anyone else, and it doesn't mean you can't enjoy basketball on a recreational level; it just means that if you truly desire to be famous, you're going to have to find another way to do it!

You must not hate who you are, and sitting around feeling sorry for yourself, focusing on your limitations, certainly won't help you be a happier person, either. If you dislike some of your own habits and the way you behave sometimes, then set out to change those things. But some things about you can't be modified, so accept what you're stuck with, so to speak, and get on with the business of being happy and successful.

What you need to say is, "Okay, I know I'll never be another Einstein, but I do have brains, and I'm going to use what I have to the best of my ability." The very best you can do is all anybody should ever ask of himself. Focus on the things you can do, and do them well, and be happy you can do what you can.

Each of us has been dealt the hand we have for a reason, and many of the things that we currently view as weaknesses, may really be strengths – we just have to learn how to apply them to our lives.

91. You have a purpose in life.

We really believe that things happen for a reason, and we also believe that everyone has a purpose in life. If you think that life is a random set of occurrences, then wake up and smell the coffee!

When you truly reflect on what has happened in your life so far, you'll see a pattern leading to where you are right now. Choices are placed before you every day, and you must decide which path you will choose. But those choices are *your* choices and not anyone else's.

Maybe you've made a series of good decisions, and you're on a path leading to happiness and fulfillment. But perhaps your life seems empty right now, and you're wondering why. It could be because of a string of bad decisions that you've made. You've probably had to face the same choices over and over, and because of stubbornness or pride or whatever reason, you've been refusing to choose what you know in your heart is the right course.

Integral to your happiness is finding that course in life which is right for you and putting all your energies in that direction. Your mission may not be easy to figure out, and it will not be the same as anyone else's, but it is essential for you to fulfill it.

Probably all of us feel somewhat insignificant at times, but that couldn't be further from the truth. When you discover what your purpose is, and you take the necessary steps to go towards that goal, you've set a plan in action which will touch hundreds, maybe even thousands of lives.

It's sad that so few ever discover what their purpose is. And, sadder still, when we realize what our mission in life is, we often spend all of our time running away from it. If you've ever read the story of Jonah in the Bible, you know that he was running away from his mission, and he got swallowed by a whale!

Fulfilling your destiny leads to true happiness, and it just might keep you from the unpleasant experience of spending time in the belly of a sea creature.

92. Stand up for your beliefs.

Sometimes when a person takes a stand, he may lose friends, or if he's in business, he may lose customers. But we mustn't let that prospect sway us, because nothing is worth compromising our principles. Our beliefs define who we are.

There's a line in an Aaron Tippin song that says, "If you don't stand for something, you'll fall for anything." And it's so true! People who are wishy-washy generally get swept away by the tide. By trying to *agree with everyone* on the larger issues of life, a person loses credibility and gains a reputation for being rather shallow. Most people, at least the ones who are worthy of our respect, will still respect us for maintaining our views even if they don't agree.

Live by the same rules, no matter where you are, and remember, "to thine own self be true." It gets too complicated if we live by different rules when we're around different people just to suit them. Pretty soon, we won't remember which face to put on around what person, and eventually, we won't even know who we are because we'll be a combination of so many different identities! If we compromise our beliefs to make others happy, we sacrifice our own happiness.

Some people are tossed around on the seas of life because they don't really know what they believe in. A person can't take a stand, if he doesn't even know where he stands.

If you don't know what you believe in and how you stand on issues, maybe you should sit down and write out your creed. Make a list of how and why you believe in the things you do. It will help define who you are and after you know that, it will be easier to enjoy your family, your job, and every area of your life.

Keeping a diary or a journal can also be helpful in this regard. It gives you a sense of consistency and continuity and helps bring what you believe in into focus for you. It helps to put your thoughts on paper. When you see things in black and white, situations often don't seem as bad.

Be yourself, and be consistent in your views.

93. Always move forward.

We should be steadfast in our beliefs, but we must not become stagnant. It's good to take time every now and then to appreciate how far we've come and think about how far we have yet to go. Evaluate your life. Do you like the direction you're going? If you do, you'll probably be happy, but you must keep on going and never rest on your past accomplishments.

If a person thinks he's in a rut or "stalled out," he's probably unhappy in almost every area of life because there's nothing worse than the feeling of going no where. We should each decide the direction we would like to go, and go there. If you can't go in that direction immediately because of financial reasons or other commitments, start to make plans to go in that direction. Situate your life so you can take that new direction. Since you only have one life, you'd better make the best of what you have.

Going into unfamiliar territory will require that you try new things, and that's good! If you're stuck in a rut, then get out and move on. Expand your comfort zone.

Lasting, positive things happen because you choose to move ahead. You decide that you won't be satisfied with just "good enough," but, instead, you want the absolute *best* for you and your family.

Keep moving. Keep dreaming. Keep living life to its fullest. Be happy.

Keep your eye on the horizon.

94. Money is important, but don't put it first in your life.

Sometimes, in our desire to move ahead, we decide that more money is the solution to our problems. More money is rarely ever the solution to any problem.

It's true that a person will be pretty unhappy if he can't even manage to pay his bills. In that regard, money *is* important. Living comfortably is definitely a reasonable goal. But going beyond the desire for adequate resources often leads to placing money as the number one desire in life, and that causes heartache and misplaced values and unhappiness.

Those of us who live with relatively modest funds, often tire of hearing the really wealthy despair of their lack of happiness. It's hard to believe that with their unlimited financial resources that they could ever have a reason to be unhappy. But it's such a common lament that there must be something to it: money simply cannot buy happiness.

Examine the things in your life which are important. Are you longing for more money because you think that would solve everything? If you are, re-examine your priorities. The desire for wealth can become a consuming passion which overshadows every other thing of lasting value.

Here's a story to illustrate the temporary nature of wealth.

A man died and went to Heaven. When he got there, he asked if he could please bring something with him. He was told that in Heaven he didn't need to bring anything because he would be provided for in every way.

He persisted in his request until St. Peter finally told him he would allow the man to bring one possession with him. The man went back and packed a suitcase full of things and returned to Heaven.

"I told you that you could bring *one* thing! Choose only one thing and leave the rest."

The man opened his suitcase and sorted through it before

finally deciding on a huge bar of pure gold. Thus prepared, he told St. Peter he was ready.

St. Peter was a little surprised at his choice. "I told you that you could bring anything you wanted into Heaven with you, and you decided to bring *asphalt*?"

There are many things which are of lasting value; money is not one of them.

Try not to take
money too seriously.

95. Give to others.

One of the best lessons to be learned from the Bible is that it is better to give than to receive. Try it sometime. If you're feeling down or unhappy, go out, find someone who is less fortunate than you, and give to them. The feeling you get when you give is happiness.

Be generous with your time, money and other resources. Learning how to let go of your money by giving it to worthy causes and people who need it is an important lesson in happiness. It helps you realize that the true value of money lies not in how much you can accumulate for yourself, but how much you can accomplish by helping others.

You can buy all kinds of material possessions which will last only a short time and bring you limited enjoyment, but you can gain so much more in the satisfaction of knowing you've really made a difference in a situation that may have seemed hopeless until you came along.

And while giving your money can be vitally important, giving your time is perhaps even more meaningful. The most valuable thing you can ever give away is your love, and giving your time is a form of loving. While we often give our finances out of surplus, giving our time involves a sacrifice. There are always things we could be doing for ourselves and our temporary enjoyment; choosing to give to someone else instead of selfishly putting ourselves and our own interests first is a wonderful route to happiness.

We should give as we would receive, cheerfully, quickly and without hesitation, for there is no grace in a benefit that sticks to the fingers.
- Seneca

96. Be committed to a cause.

Several years ago there was a television special about people who had reached an advanced age. These folks, some of whom were 100 years old or more, shared their secrets for a long and happy life.

You might think that eating right or a healthy lifestyle would be at the top of the list. Instead, there were four common themes which came as a result of conversations with these senior citizens.

One was optimism and another was the ability to deal with loss. (Even though most of them had out-lived spouses and even children, they still found a reason to go on with life and living.) The two other "secrets" were keeping active and having commitments.

Terry knows someone who is a perfect example of how staying active and being committed keeps a person happy.

"I have a friend who recently celebrated her 95th birthday. Her name is Pauline Pond, and she is one of the happiest, most contented people I know.

"Her mind has always been active and alert, but she reached a point where she was unable to get around on her own, and she became mostly confined to a wheelchair. When her husband died, she had little choice but to move from their home into a facility where she could receive 24-hour care, so she's been in a nursing home for the past several years.

"Instead of being dissatisfied with her situation, she set out to enjoy her surroundings and bring joy into the lives of others. Shortly after moving into the nursing home, she wrote a poem titled 'This Is My Home' which praised the facility and its staff and expressed her gratitude for being able to go to such a place which would care for her and provide for her needs.

"She had been a school teacher for several years, and even when she was well into her sixties, she taught music at the rural elementary school I attended. She had also been my Sunday

School teacher when I was very young. Her love for God and appreciation of music is something she has carried with her always.

"In the Christmas letter I received from her this year, she's still expressing love and appreciation. She says, ' . . . the staff is attentive, competent, helpful and works hard at making me comfortable . . . My wheelchair gives me mobility to move around the facility and with that I am able to play the piano in the dining room and do so regularly in Sunday Services and weekly singings . . .'

"The staff loves Pauline, and she continues to bring joy into the lives of all who know her. And it's because she chooses to remain as active as she can and to help others. In short, she *chooses to be happy.*"

In being active and committed to a cause, one may choose to do something which is either on a national or a local level. The idea is to get involved in something you think will make a difference in life. Feeling that you have contributed to a greater cause can help make you happier because it will bring you a sense of satisfaction knowing you have made the world a better place to live.

Wandering aimlessly for your whole life is a waste of time and is not conducive to happiness. Find something worthwhile to do, even if it seems like a very small thing, and do it!

97. Recognize lost causes, and don't continue devoting time to them.

As harsh as it may sound, some things – even projects which may have started out as positive – are not worthy of our time and attention. It is of utmost importance to help where and when we can, but we can't run ourselves into the ground chasing after every cause that comes along.

We've all had lost causes, and they are often painful to abandon because most of us don't like to give up on anyone or anything. But if we want to be happy, we have to learn to recognize what is a lost cause, and deal with it on that level. Time and energy spent on projects which are going nowhere can be better spent on different causes.

Hanging onto a lost cause can be time-consuming and dangerous. We saw an old news clipping once of a blimp going up in the air before its scheduled departure. There were people at the end of the ropes trying to hold it down, but it kept going higher and higher. While some people let go early and fell to safety, others held on, thinking they could make a difference. The blimp continued to go higher until it was obvious to all watching that it was a lost cause. But it wasn't obvious to the ones hanging onto the ropes. They held on as long as they could, and when they could no longer hold on, they fell to their deaths.

You may say to yourself, "I would never hold onto that blimp like those people." Maybe you would, and maybe you wouldn't, but that's not the issue. The question you need to ask yourself is, "Do I have any blimps in my life that I am hanging onto *right now*?" If the answer is "yes" then maybe you should let go before they go too high.

Some things are just never meant to come to pass. Clinging to these doomed projects will eventually lead to heartache and disappointment. Recognize lost causes, and eliminate them from your life.

98. Always live by the Golden Rule.

Do unto others as you would have them do unto you.

If every reasonable and sane person in the world lived by this one simple rule, there would be no unkindness or crime or unhappiness of any kind. It's an intriguing thought isn't it?

Think about how our individual lives would be different if we all adhered to this philosophy. We don't like people repeating unkind and untrue things about us, so we'd stop gossiping and spreading rumors. We would have only words of praise for those around us. We would never yell at anyone in anger or initiate or even participate in arguments.

We don't enjoy listening to friends and family constantly complain about their health and circumstances and every little detail of their lives, so we'd never again utter another griping word in the presence of anyone.

We don't like having our best ideas shot down immediately, so if we didn't happen to agree with someone, we would find a way to offer constructive criticism or we might even just keep quiet. We would be constantly encouraging others.

We don't enjoy having our every move and motive scrutinized and dissected, so we would stop obsessing about what other people think about us. We wouldn't question their reasons for doing what they do or suspect that they have ulterior motives. But since it does make us sad to know that people hate us, we would always make every effort to love everyone, hold them in the highest regard and defend their dignity and integrity at every turn.

It's hard to conceive that life could be this way, but it *is possible*, and, furthermore, what's it going to hurt to try? Don't do anything that you wouldn't want done to you, and you'll be so much happier!

When we don't treat others as we wish to be treated, we'll discover that "what goes around comes around." We're only going to get back what we put into any relationship, good or bad. So, if we dish out unpleasantness, we shouldn't be surprised when bad things come back to us.

In addition, how we treat others in life is how we are referred to in life. We don't think anyone sets out at the beginning of his life to be totally unpleasant and difficult to work with, but once he's started consistently behaving that way, that's the reputation he gets. Others begin to think of him in those terms and often treat him the same way in return, and the person who probably never intended to be unpleasant only becomes unhappier as the years go by, perpetuating the cycle by making those he comes in contact with miserable.

We should all try to take a fresh approach in dealing with those around us to make sure we're treating them as we wish to be treated.

*If King Kong had learned to live by
the Golden Rule a little earlier in his
life, things might have turned out
differently for him!*

99. Keep the faith.

Up until now, we haven't made a lot of direct references to faith, but almost all of the principles we've set forward are really spiritual ideas, many of them are concepts straight from the Bible.

It has been our observation and experience that our Creator has set up a plan for us all to achieve happiness, and He has given us a road map to get there. Look at it any way you want, rationalize if you must, but true happiness comes from a source higher than ourselves.

Of almost all of the truly happy, consistently successful and well-adjusted people we know, there are very few who are not believers. They may not all fit into the traditional *religious* molds which society has invented over the years (some of them aren't even regular church-goers), but it is their sincere desire to live their lives according to a purpose based on truth and unconditional love.

They've realized that God isn't interested in beating us down or taking the enjoyment from our lives. Instead, He has created so many good things He wants to give us, it's beyond comprehension! He wants each and every one of us to be happy, and He has the plan that will allow us the freedom to achieve happiness.

When your mindset is on the things above – things of eternal importance – minor setbacks and the daily disturbances of life have far less effect on you. You start seeing what's really important and what is not important at all.

A PRAYER

Lord, make me an instrument of Thy peace.
   Where there is hatred . . . let me sow love.
Where there is injury . . . pardon.
   Where there is doubt . . . faith.
Where there is despair . . .hope.
   Where there is darkness . . . light.
Where there is sickness . . . joy.
   O Divine Master, grant that I may not
   so much seek
To be consoled . . . as to console,
   To be understood . . . as to understand.
To be loved . . . as to love.
   For it is in giving . . . that we receive;
It is in pardoning . . . that we are pardoned;
   It is in dying . . . that we are born to
   eternal life.

ST. FRANCIS OF ASSISI

Conclusion

If you like what you've read, and you would like to be happier every day . . .

decide there
will be no
more business
as usual!

We hope that we've made it clear that we believe happiness is an attitude and a state of mind. By experience, we know that each of us can choose to be happy or choose to be unhappy.

We also hope that you will decide that you *deserve* to be happy, and that you *will be happy*. Determine that no one is going to cause you to be unhappy, and that you will do everything you can to bring joy into your own life by bringing joy into the lives of others.

As we've written this book and prepared the presentation that we do, we've often thought, "Doesn't all of this go without saying? Doesn't everyone already know that this is the stuff that makes them happy?"

After we've discussed it and thought about it, we've decided that probably deep down inside almost everyone does already know these things. Many of you who read this book are practicing them already, and maybe for others this was a "refresher course." Many other readers will know that what we're saying makes sense and may even get excited about making a change in their lives, but will take it no further.

But if you become inspired by reading or hearing this or any other message, we encourage you to let your life be changed at the moment of that inspiration. Take the message which inspires you and live a happier life.

If you have truly been inspired, you'll find it difficult to live life in your usual way and expect to be happy. You just won't be satisfied because once your mind, soul and heart have been touched with the realization that your life can be better than it's ever been before, there's no turning back.

The final point we'd like to make is that happiness does not always equal satisfaction. People can often manage to be happy even in the worst circumstances, but if one simply is not satisfied with his job or some other aspect of his life, he may need to change that part of his life where satisfaction is lacking. Life is too short to do something that you truly do not enjoy doing – something which you've merely convinced yourself that you can tolerate.

The bottom line is that each of us must take action to be consistently happy *and* satisfied in our lives. The most important thing we have to say to you in this regard is this: decide that right now, from this day forward, there will be ***no more business as usual for you!***

Resolve that you will make the changes in your life which are necessary for your happiness, and begin immediately to do so.

We'll be pulling for you all the way, because you deserve only the best in life – you deserve to be happy.

We grow by dreams. All big men are dreamers. They see things in the soft haze of a spring day, or in the red fire of a long winter's evening. Some of us let these great dreams die, but others nourish and protect them, nurse them through bad days till they bring them to the light which comes always to those who sincerely hope that their dreams will come true.

- Woodrow Wilson

Ronnie Harper and Terry Hampton have been a team since 1991 when they performed together as Petruchio and Kate in Shakespeare's *Taming of the Shrew*. After that, they appeared together in numerous plays and presentations and as masters of ceremony at various events. Over the years, they've developed a solid working relationship, as well as a strong friendship.

From their relationship, was born this book and the motivational presentations which they have done for the past several years. They have several unique and uplifting presentations to target different groups and organizations, and they seek to entertain as well as encourage – to provide lots of laughs and still give their audiences something to think about.

Drawing on the successes in their own careers, the presentations they've developed focus on the day-to-day decisions which have brought happiness into their own lives and the lives of their friends and families. While making no great claims to have all the answers, they seek to provide a balanced view of life through the use of many characters they've created over the years. Using costumes and props, their standard presentation is lively and fast-paced and probably different than anything you've seen before.

If you're looking for a more traditional program, they're also available individually to speak on a variety of topics. Regardless of the approach, they promise to entertain, motivate, encourage and provide a gentle reminder of the things that are truly important in life.

Ronnie and Terry are available to speak at churches, teachers' meetings and for a variety of other groups and organizations. For information on obtaining them to speak at your next event, contact them at the following address:

FELLOW TRAVELLERS
P.O. Box 1102
West Plains, MO 65775

About the Authors

Ronnie Harper and Terry Hampton

Terry Hampton was born and raised in West Plains, Missouri. She was active in many clubs and organizations during high school and was named Girls' Best Citizen her senior year. During her speech and debate career at West Plains High School, she won numerous awards and went to nationals in extemporaneous speaking. After graduation, she attended Southwest Missouri State University, married the fabulous Allen Hampton (her husband of eighteen years), and managed to give birth to the most wonderful child in the universe – Tracy Eran – who is a college freshman. She continues to be active in the community and was named West Plains "Woman of the Year" in 1990 and "Volunteer of the Year" in 1995. She enjoys community theatre, walking, reading, going to auctions and attempting to maintain a garden.

Ronnie Harper was raised in West Plains, Missouri. He participated in many activities in school including football, track, band, choir, National Honor Society, and student council just to name a few. He attended Arkansas State University on a tuba scholarship, and that is where he met Tammie (his wife of ten years). After changing majors a few times, he decided on and graduated with his B.S.E. Ronnie has taught adaptive physical education and special education K-12, and has appeared in Arkansaw Traveler productions during summer break. Currently, Ronnie and his wife are employed by the West Plains School District – Tammie as a Speech Pathologist, Ronnie as a high school learning disabilities and behavior disorder teacher. His hobbies include community theatre, hunting, and collecting things that interest him.

Our Notes of Thanks

I thank my wonderful husband and beautiful daughter for being the most fun a family could be. I think of all of the times we've laughed until we cried over the oddest things, of our hopes and dreams as individuals and as a family, and how we've managed to work through all of life's challenges by loving each other, and when I think of those things, I can't imagine my life without the two of you. I thank God for you both.

Thanks Mom and Dad for supporting me in everything I've ever done. You loved the poems I wrote as a child and thought my stories were beyond compare. I know that being a happy adult is the result of having a childhood full of love.

So many friends and family members have been instrumental in helping me be where I am right now. The late Lisa Truehart gave me my first opportunity to be on stage doing live theatre, and the experience has forever changed the course of my life. Judy B., I'm so glad you're my friend. And to Ronnie, what can I say? You're the best! I don't have room to thank everyone individually who's touched my life in a positive way, but I love and appreciate every one of you.

Finally, I thank my heavenly Father, His son Jesus and the Holy Spirit for life, light, and love beyond measure. The way God has orchestrated the circumstances in my life is continually awe-inspiring to me.

- Terry

Where does a person start whose life has been touched by so many people? I guess I should start at the beginning, with my parents. Mom and Dad, thanks for providing me a home which was more than food and shelter. A place so rich with love and caring that I didn't realize we were poor when I was growing up until a few years ago. Thank you for everything; a kid couldn't ask for better parents. Thanks to all my teachers. Thanks Mrs. Dana Johnston for listening and caring, Mrs. Kelly Dame for touching my life with music and for giving me some great advice at a time in my life when I needed it and thanks to both of them for showing me it's okay to be crazy. Thanks to Dr. Tom Adams and to Dr. Cindy Albright for your inspiration. Thanks to Lisa Truehart for helping me cultivate my love and respect for the stage and for helping me become an actor. Thanks to Terry Hampton for showing me what a "doer" is and for being a great friend, acting partner, business partner and fellow traveller. I wouldn't have come this far without your help and I'm looking forward to the rest of our trip together. To Judy Bowles for being my friend. Your friendship, support and encouraging words mean so much to me. Thanks to Leslie Harper, my niece, for helping me rediscover the wonders and joys of life as seen from your innocent perspective. I want to thank God for all the things that seem like just coincidences but are really your hand leading me down this road we call life. Thanks to Laura Greaves, Russell Decker, Sandy and Bailey Laymen, Gary Reed, Grayson Gordon, Dee Dungan, Rodney and Cindy Harper, Tracie Dungan, all my grandparents and the rest of my family and friends too numerous to mention. And finally, I want to thank Tammie, my wife, for putting up with my crazy ideas, and projects. First you were my friend, then my lover and now my life. Thanks for your love and support, they mean more than I could ever say.

- Ronnie

There is no duty we so much underrate as the duty of being happy. By being happy we sow anonymous benefits upon the world.

- Robert Louis Stevenson